Called From the Abyss

Martial arts expert Nico the Dragon was lost in the darkness. Until he heard the voice ...

by Nicholas Hill
with
Ken Wade

All events portrayed in this work are based on the memory of the author, Nicholas Hill. For personal reasons some details have been modified slightly and some names have been substituted.

Cover Design: Ken Wade, Holly Anderson

ISBN: 0692458778
ISBN-13: 978-0692458778

DEDICATION

Dedicated to Tad Caviness, one of God's soldiers. You fought the good fight, buddy. Can't wait to meet you in heaven.

ACKNOWLEDGMENTS

To list all the people who have been an encouragement and aided me in my journey would take several pages. This book could not have come into reality without their help.

Among those who have helped me bring God's Soldier Ministries to sharp focus, I must mention Pastor Larry Meager, Pastor Larry Caviness, Pastor Rick Roethler, Pastor Gerard Kiemeney, and the entire staff of the Southern California Conference of Seventh-day Adventists. You had a vision of what this ministry could become long before I did.

Holly Anderson, you have stood beside me and done so much for the ministry and me personally. You are my Lady of the Light. Surely you have laid up abundant treasure in heaven.

Eric Edmunds, you and your family gave me shelter in a time of need.

Michael Barbar and Pat Andrakin, you two were my Caleb and Joshua in the early days of reaching out to share my story. Thank you for being men of faith, along with Eric Flickenger and all the others at AFCOE. GiGi Erneta, thank you for your exemplary spiritual walk and your willingness to be involved in ministry.

John Villa and Chaplain Cedric Brown, thank you for opening the doors to enable me to touch the lives of so many young people from troubled backgrounds.

Pastor Augie Barajas and the entire staff at Victory Outreach—you have helped me find my true self and my true voice in more ways than you can imagine. Dr. Douglas Nies, you walked with me through some of the darkest parts of my life and encouraged me to keep looking to the light. Pastor Danny Chan, your encouragement means much to me.

Craig Dinkel, you believed in me, in spite of myself. Steve Langa, you listened to my confused words and helped me see the light in them.

Christopher Hunt, Benny Urquidez, Jeff Langton, Matt

Burch, Shark Fralick, and Forest Henry, you fighters were always in my corner, even when I was down for the count. Thank you!

Dr. Kevin Roberts and the staff at Glendale Adventist Hospital, without your support and help with my medical issues, I would not have been able to move forward in ministry.

Both my father John and mother Barbara have played important roles in my life, of course. Thank you Dad, and also Yvonne, for your supportive attitude and actions as I have come out of the darkness into the light. Brother Danny, I appreciate the encouragement you and your family continue to bring.

Last but not least I must mention Ken Wade who poured countless hours into finding and telling my story. His spiritual discernment and God-given gifts have brought my journey to life in a way that lifts up and magnifies God's power to transform and restore lives.

Thanks be to God for all of you and the countless others whose lives have empowered my life and continue to do so.

CONTENTS

Chapter 1

I stared into the mirror, unsure what I was seeing. I blinked, looked away, then swung my face back around, almost expecting to see a demon staring back from the spit-smeared, cracked glass.

But it was the same face.

A strange face. Who was it?

I squinted, rubbed the cheek of the person staring back at me, and a white powder left a residue on my fingers.

I was looking at a dead man, and the dead man was all there was left of who I used to be.

Finally! I thought.

Finally!

The day I had longed for, the day I had dreamed of, the day I had poured my soul, my heart, my every waking moment into seeking for a decade had arrived, and I would not be tormented any more, ever again.

At least not on this earth.

Sure I might meet my demons again—the demons that had driven me to want to destroy myself, spoken to me from shop windows as I walked the dark streets of Koreatown, Los Angeles, peering into the eyes of each person I met, striking fear into some, seeing invitations to evil in others, and scaring evil intent out of others.

But in hell they would have to respect me. They couldn't just stare into my eyes, stare through the lobes of my brain down to where my soul writhed in pain that would only end when my heart stopped its incessant pounding. Never again would I take orders from them, orders telling me to hurt myself, to take all the rage that had built up inside me through years of abuse as a child and hard living as an adult, and hurt myself with it.

I had had respect at one time. In the boxing ring, in the Mixed-Martial Arts world, the business world, in Hollywood. But now I didn't even respect myself. Would I ever be respected again?

My heart, the heart of a warrior, was fighting me now, just like everything else in the world seemed to be. But it kept up its incessant beating in my chest. It wouldn't quit! Why wouldn't it quit? Maybe today, finally it would! Maybe it would explode, and the detonation would be the last bit of pain I felt. It seemed to want to beat its way out of my chest, and I hoped it would.

Yes! Heart do it! Pound your way out. Explode! End this pain! I can't take it anymore. Send me straight to hell, and there I will deal with my demons, and they will have to sit up and listen; I will no longer have to listen to their taunts and temptations, because nobody—nobody on this earth—dares to treat Nico the Dragon with disrespect.

Nico the Dragon, that was my name, and that was my reputation when, as a mixed-martial-arts cage fighter, I pounded man after man into submission in vicious, unregulated, underground fights amidst the adulation of cheering crowds who lusted for blood and cheered me on and lauded me with gifts, praise, wine, women, and song because I was the toughest kid on the block.

There's a story about Nico the Dragon that I'm not proud of today, but I want you to know something about the man I was looking at in the mirror—or the specter I was looking at in the mirror. That pale, white, skeletal face looking back at me with red eyes and blood dripping from a nose burned out by snorting crystal meth was no more than a shadow of the face that had once glared at the world from movie posters and fight banners and stared down pimps, johns, pushers, and abusers of every stripe.

Just the name Nico the Dragon had once been enough

to gain admission to L.A.'s toniest clubs. Every bouncer at every club that was a must-go place for those who wanted to see and be seen in the glitziest, most plastic city on earth, knew my name and my reputation, and if I and my entourage wanted to move to the front of the line of people stringing halfway down the block hoping and praying for admission, nobody would stand in my way, and nobody would try to stop me. At the door, it would be "Hey Nico, you're in bro." And the cute, hopeful starlets in sparkly mini-dresses, shivering in the chill of a January night, or perspiring in the heat of October's Santa Ana winds could only stare with jealous eyes and dream that one night they might be the piece of eye candy on my arm, and get some respect.

Some say the highest form of praise is imitation. But in actuality there is a higher form. When someone tries to move through the world—push their way through the world—using your reputation.

I encountered that phenomenon one night at a pool table at one of Hollywood's hottest destinations.

A few friends and I were playing pool, having a good time, laughing, drinking, making an impression on the gorgeous girls we'd picked up at the bar, when a big, mean-looking dude with 'tude lumbered up, followed by his own entourage, and began to try to stare us down. Like he wanted to take over the table.

I hardly glanced at him. My friends and I just kept playing. After five minutes of trying to intimidate us off the table, the guy walked right up, picked up our cue ball, and dumped it in a pocket. "Your game's over!" he announced.

One of my friends, no small fellow himself, went up to him, looked him right in the eye, and said as calmly as he could, "Hey, what you doin' man? We got a game goin' here, we got good money on it, and we're not done."

"Yeah, you are."

"Why's that?"

"Because I said so."

"Who are you?"

"You wanna find out who I am here, or out on the street?"

"What's that supposed to mean?"

The big guy bent over, glaring into my friend's eyes, and whispered in his ear "You wanna know who I am?"

My friend nodded. "Yeah, I do."

"Well, I'm Nico the Dragon, and nobody messes with Nico the Dragon. Got it?"

My friend just nodded and came over to talk to me.

Now, I've had training in acting.

I've been in about 20 movies, mainly as a martial-arts fighter with people like Pat Morita of *Karate Kid* fame, Danny Trejo, Timothy Bottoms, and Pamela Anderson. I'd even appeared in an episode of the *Drew Carey Show*, and had my own show on the Spike Network at one time.

So I know how to put on a face, put on an act, and I decided I wanted to have some fun with this guy.

My eyes went wide. My jaw dropped. My face flushed with excitement, and I walked over to this big guy. I'm six-foot-three, but I slouched a little, made myself look smaller, so that I could look up at him, and I put a little bit of an ironic smile on my lips. "You're Nico the Dragon?" I said, feigning awe.

"Yeah. So what?"

"I mean, like, wow! I just always wanted to meet Nico the Dragon."

"Move on, buddy."

"I've heard that you have these really cool dragon tattoos on your arms."

He wasn't even looking at me now, just ignoring me the way celebrities treat drooling fans.

"I mean, I just wonder if I could see them."

He turned my way, deigning for a brief moment to cast his gaze upon his pathetic groupie. "No. You can't."

I pulled myself out of my slouch and stood to my full height, locking my eyes on his.

"You're not Nico the Dragon," I said quietly. But he wouldn't blink. He continued to try to intimidate me. With our eyes still daring each other's to look away, I rolled up the left sleeve of my clubbing shirt, then the right sleeve.

"Who says I'm not?"

"I say you're not."

"Who are you?"

When you go into the boxing ring or into the MMA cage with an opponent, you want to terrify him, want to make him doubt himself and wish he'd never gotten in there with you, and tattoos can help you do that. A bulging chest can help. Rippling biceps deliver a message. But it's the eyes that make all the difference. It's how you look at the man that tells him he doesn't scare you, and he'd better be scared of you. Your look tells him that if he drops his stare for one split second, the fight's as good as over.

He was a fighter. I could tell that. Because he wouldn't drop his eyes. So I slowly, ever so slowly, moved mine downward, letting him know I was not looking away from him, but looking where I wanted to look, and when I did that, his eyes followed mine, and when he saw the dragons on my arms, something changed in his eyes.

"I was just wondering if Nico's tats look anything like these," I said.

He just stared, trying hard not to show fear. He no doubt had seen videos of me pounding guys a lot tougher than him into bloody submission. Maybe he'd even been in the crowd shouting, egging me on to deliver ever more pain to an opponent who just wouldn't quit until I had nearly beaten the life out of him with my bare fists.

His mouth came open, but no words came out, so I leaned forward so my lips were right up against his ear, and I whispered, "Now, I don't want to embarrass you in front of your friends here, so why don't you just buy me and my friends drinks for the rest of the night, and let us finish our game. My favorite bartender's right over there," I pointed to him. "Don't forget to leave a good tip, and we'll pretend this never happened."

My friends and I had drinks on him for the rest of the night.

You just didn't disrespect Nico the Dragon, no matter who you were. It just wouldn't be a smart thing to do, not if you knew my reputation. Even if you didn't know my reputation, I had a way of carrying myself that said "Mess with this at your peril." It wasn't the tough, mean-guy persona that you might imagine, it was just a way of walking with power. If you'd seen me on the TV news doing an interview before a fight, or seen me on Spike TV where I'd had my own show for a while, you'd have seen a grinning, affable, handsome, likable guy that you might sit down to coffee with and shoot the breeze, tell funny stories, and have a good laugh, slap each other on the back while shaking hands, and walk away with a jaunty step, smiling at the world.

That was me at one time, before the demons got the upper hand.

Sure, take me to hell, I thought. I'll teach you something about respect there.

The reason I was standing, staring at my skeletal remains in the mirror, was because the demons had told me my time had arrived, my goal (their goal for me) had been achieved, my usefulness to them on earth was at an end, and it was my time. Today was my day to die and join them in hell.

I needed to see that reflected in the mirror.

I had been watching myself descending into hell for years. Literally watching, observing the signs of my own progression into nothingness, my descent into the abyss.

If you had visited me in my room minutes earlier (not that I probably would have let you in), you would have seen me sitting on the floor amidst scraps and detritus of my own destroyed life and others' as well. Bits of torn clothing, half-eaten burgers, broken bongs and meth pipes, containers with fries and a bit of dried-up ketchup in the bottom. Anything I saw on the littered streets around my home that spoke to me, I would pick up and bring back, and it would never leave. The floor just kept getting deeper and deeper with trash, bits and pieces of others' meaningless lives as well as my own.

What furniture there was—an old table, a roll-away bed, a few tattered chairs, were blood-spattered. Beneath the table an old computer hummed, and on the table were several monitors, only one of which was still functional. The others had had their faces punched in—my face punched in, really—and bits of broken glass was all that was left of the screen that used to tell me my own story.

I had a webcam that I would point at myself to document, for my own eyes only, the descent of a somewhat-sober human being into the depraved depths of a crystal meth high. For some reason I wanted to watch it happen, and I would stare at the screen as my drug of choice sped through my body, robbing me of the power of rational thought, taking me to a place where I could not feel pain. But at times I so loathed the person I saw on the screen that my fist—the one I had used to bloody many another man's face—would literally punch my own lights out. My fists are still lightning-fast, and they could punch through a computer screen without a second's thought. Sure they'd be bloody and painful afterwards, but that was nothing new to me. The walls of my room bore testimony to that with a dozen or more blood-rimmed holes that I had punched through solid plaster and the wooden lath behind it. My landlord had tried many times to evict me, but that's a story for another time.

As I sat there on the floor that day, the demons visited me again.

I don't know how to explain it to someone who has never experienced it. You may think that I was only hallucinating—that because of all the drugs I had done in my life, the countless blows I had taken to my head, my macerated mind was somehow split, and I perceived the voices that spoke to me from within my head as literal beings separate from me.

You can think that if you want. But to me they were as real as any human being I had met. In a chair beside me, staring down at me with hollow, soulless eyes, sat a stripper, barely clothed, her legs crossed, her right foot kicking, almost spasming in frustration, perhaps rage. On an old, torn couch lounged a fat pusher, leering at me in his fancy duds.

Both of them had expectations of me.

He was angry at me, she was scornful.

He roused himself and sat up, leaning forward, elbows on his knees, and spoke quietly. "You see, the thing is Nico, we got no more use for you on this planet. Your time is up, your day has come. This is what you've been waiting for, and we're here to help you—to accelerate you, to push the pedal to the metal for you. You see, you're no good to us anymore, because you're working against us, really. When you go out on the streets at night and try to protect young kids—keep them from getting beat up, or from getting messed up like you. You even protect hookers. Well, that's not what we're all about my friend. And we can't use you no more. Who do you think you are? You're the dragon. And today is the day you become extinct."

This is it! I thought. Yes! Finally my day has come. My day to die.

I had often thought of killing myself, and only one thing had stopped me from taking a gun and blowing my brains out.

I didn't want to leave a mess for other people to have to clean up.

I didn't want my brother and my two little nieces to be left with a picture in their mind of Nico with a hole in his face and his brains splattered all over the wall. So I'd chosen a slower way to kill myself, with drugs. Not that what I was doing was any more dignified, but at least they wouldn't be left with that mind picture.

My day had finally arrived, and I needed to see what that looked like. So I got up off the floor and went to my door. I lived in two rooms of a six-room apartment on the second floor of a decrepit brick building on the edge of Los Angeles's Koreatown. Much of the lower floor was uninhabitable. The owner had long-since quit paying the mortgage, and quit maintaining the place. I (supposedly) rented all six rooms, but was letting two other derelicts stay in the other bedrooms. None of us actually paid rent, yet we hadn't been evicted, but that—as I said—is a story for another time.

I struggled to my feet like a punch-drunk boxer and stumbled to the door, fumbled with the two chain locks and finally got them undone, then headed down the hall to the bathroom the three of us shared, but no one ever cleaned.

And that's where I saw the ghost.

I don't know if you're supposed to be able to see ghosts in a mirror or not, but that's what I was looking at. A mere phantom of the man I had once been.

I wasn't literally a ghost, you understand, because according to the lore of such things, ghosts can pass straight through walls or glass or mirrors. I know I wasn't a ghost, because when I took my head and slammed it into the mirror, head-butting myself like a cage opponent, the mirror broke, and bits of glass imbedded themselves in my forehead, and blood began to run into my eyes, obscuring my vision of myself.

That made me angry. And despite my weakened condition, anger could still find its way to my fists.

Tattooed on the knuckles of my right fist in big, bold letters is the word TAKE, and tattooed on the left fist is THAT. You look at me with my knuckles raised, and you get the message TAKE THAT! And if you know anything about my background, or have ever watched me throw a punch, you know what THAT is.

THAT went into the mirror, shattering what remained of it. Then I turned to the frosted-glass window on my left, and TAKE shot through it, gaining its own baptism of blood.

Pain raged through my body. I lashed out at everything in sight, then staggered down the hall, back to my room, dripping blood.

I had a cat.

A black cat.

She had watched me descend into the horror show that I now was, and would still rub up against my legs and purr ever-so-sweetly like I was the most worthy person in the world, and she was the one thing in my world that I did not want to hurt, so I picked her up gently in my bloody hands and put her into my other room and closed the door so that she would not have to witness what was about to happen.

Now I stood to my full height. Ready to face the enemy head on and look him in the eye.

"It's about to happen!" The voice came from inside my head. "It's about to happen! You're going to look the monster—the devil—in the eye, and you're going to spit in his eye, and then you're going to die. It's about to happen!"

I looked wildly around the room, and I could see in my mind's eye all the monsters who had come to torment me there, glaring at me. And that's when it hit me. I realized that I was the biggest, worst monster in the room. It should have made me happy. Should have made me smile with a sense of satisfaction and accomplishment. I had become what I had set out to be.

But instead of satisfaction I felt hatred. I hated what I had become, and I flew into a rage again, smashing everything.

Barefoot I began to stomp on the broken glass pipes on the floor—pipes that had been the delivery tools of my addictions. But there were two really nice ones, and somehow I had the presence of mind to set them aside where I would not destroy them, because they were calling to me, speaking to me, telling me that they were there to deliver that last and final dose that would liberate me from the life I so despised.

Finally, a bloody and bleeding mess, I fell to my knees and picked up one of the glass pipes, ready at last to leave the world.

The voices were speaking to me, telling me that it was time to take that last dose. "Do it! Hurry! Do as much as you can as fast as you can!" That is what they had been saying to me for the last ten years, but today they spoke even louder, with even more urgency! "Do it Nico! Slay the dragon at last!"

"I'm doing it as fast as I can!" I yelled back in frustration.

But then another voice, quiet but insistent amid the cacophony, tried to make itself heard. It was a voice I'd heard before. Even as I tried to silence all rational thought with drugs, it had not given up.

It was just a whisper at first, but as I knelt there, it grew louder and louder.

"Is this what you want, then, Nico? For them to find you, just another burned out addict, lying on the floor, eyes staring into heaven in search of salvation you will never find, garbage on your right, garbage on your left, garbage for your bed? The demons you have fought will have won, and they will go on to more conquests. They will inhabit the lives of those who find you. Is that what you want? Really?"

And for some reason I paused on that final flight of my stairway to hell and cocked my ear to listen, and from somewhere in the haze reason broke through, and I could see clearly: that was not what I wanted.

That voice had begun to speak to me when I was just eight years old, and it had continued to speak to me through the drug-induced fog of my addiction. "I claimed you as God's Soldier, Nico. Is this the way God's Soldier is going to die?" it asked now.

Chapter 2

There were times in my life when I thought I had the world by the tail, and I could swing it or spin it any way I wanted to.

It was the summer of 2001, as I recall. Let me say this though, as you read my story, please understand that this is MY story, as well as I have been able to reconstruct it from memory and the few bits and pieces of my life—a stack of photographs mainly—that managed to stay with me through nearly a decade of decadent living, drug addiction, and bondage to unseen masters I did not even know existed.

Friends too, have helped me put some of the pieces of my past together, finding references and images of parts of my life on the Internet, and at sites like the Internet Movie Database, which lists most of the B-movies and TV shows I had roles in.

I was tooling around all the Hollywood hot spots in those days, on a tricked-out custom Harley whose fuel tank was created for me in the shape of a dragon's head. But that was only good for times I wanted to be alone, or with my riding buddies. If I wanted to take just one cute model or actress with me, my car of choice was the steel gray 2000 Corvette I'd been given by my employer.

But when I really wanted to make an impression and have room for my buddies and me to pick up girls along the way, the car of choice was The Dragon Wagon—a 1964

NICHOLAS HILL

Cadillac Coupe Deville that I had spent two years, and more money than I could have counted, in totally customizing.

When I bought the car, it was pink.

Yes, that's right, a pink Cadillac, chopped and dropped, sleek and in-your-face. When my boss first saw me pull into the lot with it, he couldn't believe his eyes. What was tough-guy Nick (he always called me Nick, not Nico) doing driving a pink Cadillac? But then he got the picture—it would take a guy like me to pull that off in Hollywood, and he really liked it. He needed people with thick skin to handle the phone lines of his telemarketing company, and he liked the idea that I wasn't going to let anybody give me guff about anything—not even driving a pink Caddy.

I had plans for that car, though, and over the next several months it went from pink to flat black to shiny black with flames raging along the sides and over the hood. Recently we found, on the Internet, a comment by the guy who owned it after me. "I remember buying this car in '01 from Nicco [sic] "The Dragon" Hill in Southern Cali. ... I bought it black with purple ghost flames, fat white walls, the rear window opening was in the shape of the 'Tapout' logo, and had a correct '64 steering wheel cut on top and bottom in the shape of a Batman symbol. Great Times! Cruising down the 405 freeway shooting 2-4 foot flames out the tailpipes."

It was a car designed to make an impression, and I'm sure it did. I didn't just have the outside redone of course. The inside was all leather, and I even had the underside of the hood and lid of the trunk painted with colorful dragon murals! In 2014, as I'm writing this book, pictures of the car can be seen on the Internet, because it's for sale in Pittsburgh, where a collector has kept it for years, using it as what he described as a "trailer-queen" show car, driving it just enough to keep it healthy, and trailering it around to display at auto shows.

I was living the high life, and thought I was king of my domain. I was making money hand over fist, and it was flowing through my fingers like water through a sieve. I

22

thought I was on top of the world, and that the good times would never quit rolling for me.

Don't get the idea, though, that I was making all that money because I was some great movie star or champion fighter. No, I had never made that kind of money even back in 1995 when half-a-dozen movies came out with my name in the credits.

The money was coming from a real job as the number-one sales-producer for a company that did millions of dollars in business every month. Our main business was creating infomercials and selling products to people who called in after watching our programs on TV, and that is where I excelled. If you've never tried to sell a $4,000 product to someone you've never met, who just called an 800 number they saw on TV, you don't know what it's like to be a high-stakes telemarketer.

A few years earlier I'd had no idea what it was like, and neither had I had any idea how to do such a thing.

In my movie roles I'd made good, but not great money. In my first two films (real low-budget flicks), I was the star, both times playing a martial-artist from some other planet. In later movies I sometimes had only smaller parts, usually involving martial arts fighting. In 1997 I'd had a small role in an important movie, and had also served as one of the stunt coordinators, along with my buddy Shark (David Fralick), who was a regular on *The Young and the Restless* in those days.

I'd also had a major role in a TV movie that was filmed in Canada, and on the set I'd met a woman I knew I wanted to marry.

I'd been married once before, to a 26-year-old model when I was only 18, but the marriage lasted less than a year. Now, at age 36, I chose an 18-year-old actress to be my wife.

Shortly after we were married, life began to imitate art for me. After years of training people in self-defense and playing the role of a fighter on the big screen, the opportunity came for me to try my hand at a genuine mixed martial arts fight at a venue in Brazil. Looking back on that time now, I wonder how I could have been so crazy. Cage fighting is a young man's game. I was 35 when I had my first professional fight—by that age I should have been planning my retirement from the sport.

My first real cage fight didn't end well for me, but it taught me a lot about the sport that came in handy in later fights that didn't end well for the other guy that went into the cage with me.

I returned from Brazil beat up, but not beaten down, and in desperate need of a steady income to support my new family. Acting gigs are always hit-and-miss unless you're on the A-list, and the only skills I really had to offer an employer were based around acting and fighting—neither of which would provide a regular pay check.

The man who would be my boss, and later my friend, at the company I applied to knew that every Monday morning when he walked into the classroom for the first session in a week-long training series, he would be looking into the eyes of a lot of desperate people. People who think they can do anything else usually don't apply for jobs in telephone sales work. Most of the applicants he met were there only because they couldn't find work anywhere else.

Myself included.

I had absolutely no experience in sales, other than selling myself to directors at auditions. But I was pretty good at that, I guess. Because when Greg (not his real name) looked at me, he thought he saw potential there.

An athlete himself, with an NCAA national swimming title on his résumé, he had a special place in his heart for men and women with the sort of edge that the need to be a winner hones in them. He welcomed me to the class, and for the next five days drilled into me and the other participants how difficult it would be to make it in the fast-paced world of selling intangible products over the telephone.

Fortunately we wouldn't be making cold calls to people who were angry at us for interrupting them in the middle of their favorite TV show. The people we talked to would be calling us for more information about our company's training programs after watching an infomercial. What we needed to try to sell them was instruction and mentoring in buying and selling commodities such as gold, silver, oats, corn, and pork bellies.

I left the classroom on Friday full of self-doubt, but willing to give it a try.

On Monday morning I reported for work in a room full of people with telephones and headsets who were already involved in conversations with potential customers. Several of the people who had gone through the training with me didn't even bother to show up that day, having taken to heart Greg's warnings about how difficult the job would be, and not wanting to risk wasting their time doing something that might not pay them a cent.

Greg had explained to us that the only way we'd be paid for showing up would be to make sales. There was no salary. It was strictly commission-based sales work.

I've never been one to give up without at least giving it my best effort, so with fear and trepidation I sat down at my work station and took my first call. I tried explaining to the potential customer how the commodities markets worked, and how our training and mentoring would help him make a killing, whether the market was headed up or down. But the gentleman on the other end just said he'd have to think about it for a while, then hung up.

A supervisor had been standing right behind me, listening to me all through the call. He frowned at me when I turned around and shrugged after losing that sale.

Bill, the man in the booth next to mine, was having a hard time making a sale, too. Each of us took several more calls that morning, but neither of us made a sale. When it came time for a lunch break, I looked around quickly, almost expecting Greg to come storming down the aisle to bawl me out and send me packing, but when I didn't see him, I got up quickly and found my way out the door and to the nearest fast-food joint for a quick burger, fries, and soda, then sneaked back into the call center and took my place.

I noticed that Bill from the next station didn't return after lunch.

At five o'clock Greg came by to see how I felt about the day. I think he expected me to be looking all discouraged and ready to quit, but when I saw him I said, "I think I'm almost there. Didn't quite get a sale, but tomorrow's another day." I flashed him my most winning smile.

He told me later that he was ready to give me my walking papers at the end of that first day. He'd actually sent Bill packing after only three hours of trying, because he could tell that he just didn't have what it took.

But he looked into my eyes and must have seen the sort of determination that I always conveyed to directors and fight opponents, and he didn't have the heart to kill my dream—yet.

To this day Greg can't explain to you why he let me keep coming back day after day, even though I had yet to make a sale. He didn't do that for anyone else. Almost everybody who had taken the training alongside me was gone before the first week was over, and Greg says that he and the supervisors discussed sending me on my way several times, but for some reason he believed in me, and believed that someday I would have a breakthrough.

His confidence eventually paid off big-time.

It took me about three weeks of failure, but by the end of that third week, with some great coaching from Greg, I had figured it out. I wasn't supposed to be selling information about commodities trading, or about our training system. I was supposed to be selling the dream of financial independence. That's what people who called were really wanting to buy.

And once I figured out that—as they put it in the sales world—you don't sell the steak, you sell the sizzle, things turned around quickly for me.

Soon I was the top sales person in the room.

If you called our toll-free number, you would first be

offered a training system costing $4,000. But if you wouldn't buy at that level, I was supposed to offer you a $3600 system, and if that wouldn't get you, I could keep lowering the level of services I sold you until we got to the bottom at a $995 package.

That's what I was instructed to do.

But I've never been particularly good at doing what I was told to do.

If I wanted to make serious money, I needed to sell the $4,000 package or nothing at all. No true fighter ever goes into the ring hoping to take second place in a fight. And I just could not get it through my head that settling for selling the second-best package was not the same thing as tapping out or admitting defeat.

So I sold the $4,000 package only, and got a 20% commission for each sale.

There would be days when Greg would come to me near the end of the day and say, "Nick, we need just a couple more sales to meet a quota today. Whatever call you take next, I want you to not let them go. Make a sale even if you have to go down to the sixth tier. Got it, buddy?"

"Got it, boss," I'd say. But he could see in my eyes that I wasn't going to do what he said.

"Please, just this once, Nick. We gotta get a sale, any sale in the next hour, or we won't meet quota."

I'd just wink at him and go back to my station, leaving him shaking his head in frustration.

And every single time that happened, I would deliver him a $4,000 sale before the time was up. I never once backed down from my all-or-nothing standard, and never once missed the deadline.

So you can see why I thought I had the world on a string, and that I could swing and spin it around my head at will.

My paycheck at the end of each week would usually be somewhere around $4,000 or $5,000. And it was all good, honest, hard-earned money. When I talked to Greg recently, he reminded me that there were certain sales people in the same room who would resort to all sorts of fabrications to close a deal, but Greg was always impressed by the fact that I didn't feel the need to do that. All my sales tactics were totally above board. I might have been selling dreams, but at least I was doing it honestly.

Honest and hard-working were two traits I brought to the table. Unfortunately I didn't bring another trait or skill that I really needed: the ability to handle money wisely.

Like clockwork I'd be back at my station every Monday morning, flat broke and needing to sell another five or ten programs just to keep bread on the table at home and gas in my car.

My new young wife soon tired of me. I was working long hours and partying longer hours, and she soon moved out and asked for a divorce. Which didn't save me a single penny, because now I could spend every night partying, as well as the weekends.

After about three years in that high-pressure sales environment, though, I was burning out. It wasn't nearly as much fun anymore. I was still making really good money, but I wasn't having nearly as much fun.

Sure, as a favorite of the CEO and COO, I was given plenty of perks—trips to Vegas and Aspen and other great places on the corporate jets, hob-knobbing with the rich and famous. But I had to drag myself to my work station every day, and I often would be day dreaming when my phone would ring, and would have to drag myself back into the real world and try to make another sale.

The CEO could see that I was burning out, but he didn't seem to want to lose me. I'm not sure why. He had noticed that I had a lot of friends and powerful connections in Hollywood, so it could be that he wanted to keep me around to open doors and give credibility to our company, which was investing big bucks in trying to profit from the Internet dot-com boom.

As the company expanded into new endeavors and bought up smaller companies, the CEO took me off my sales desk and gave me a fancy title in one of the new branches. To be honest with you I can't even remember what my title was, but it was pretty high up the executive ladder. The title was useful. It boosted my ego, which didn't really need any fortification, but it moved me into a position I was totally unqualified for. That didn't really bother me though, it was the perks I liked. And one of my favorites was the Corvette.

It wasn't like giving me a $50,000 car as a bonus was going to break the company up in business. But then one day when I drove up to the office and parked in my reserved spot and went in, my assistant told me the boss wanted to see me.

"I need the keys to the Corvette," he told me.

"What? Why?"

"Other people were promised cars, too, and due to some setbacks in the transition, they didn't get them. They're jealous, Nick. We've got to return the car to the dealer."

It wasn't my only car, so it's not like it left me without wheels, but it was like a blow to the solar plexus to have that beautiful machine taken away so suddenly and unceremoniously.

I might be the toughest kid on the block, but that didn't mean I was on the top of the heap when it came to corporate politics.

Little did I know how far I was from the top, how little control I really had of my life. That lesson would be driven home hard and fast in the coming days.

And in the coming years I would have some really tough lessons to learn about who's really in charge of something even bigger than corporate America—the whole world.

Chapter 3

Losing the keys to my beloved Corvette was certainly not the first step in a downhill direction for me, but it was a wakeup call.

You know how you can be walking along on what you think is level ground, not really paying attention to where you set your feet, and then all of a sudden there's a little dip—maybe just a couple inches—and you step down unexpectedly, and it throws you off balance, maybe throws your back out of kilter or trips you up, and all of a sudden you realize you need to pay attention to where you're stepping?

Something like that happened to me on a movie set once. Some of my martial-arts buddies and I had already shot several fast-paced scenes where we were bouncing off each other like billiard balls, throwing punches, round-house kicks, all sorts of really physical stuff. I was feeling on the top of my game, having a great time. Then the next day I was supposed to do a simple walk-and-talk scene with Frank Shamrock, and while we were walking I came to one of those dips—maybe a curb, or a step, I don't really remember what. Anyhow the step down caught me by surprise, and a loud pop emanated from my knee, and an electric shockwave shot up my leg and through my back, and I crumpled to the ground, rolling in pain. Next thing I knew, I was on the operating table, undergoing surgery to repair a knee that had finally paid the price of years of hard use. The doctor who repaired it said it was like trying to put a shattered soda bottle back together again.

That was a wakeup call that warned me to watch where I was going. There's a larger power, called gravity, constantly working in the background, and even though you think you're flying high and untouchable, gravity has a way of always bringing you back down to earth.

Realizing that didn't keep me from ever daring to walk again, of course. But it did humble me. I wasn't quite as invincible as I thought I was.

Despite the knee injury I was back in the MMA cage fighting again, way too soon, having to learn the lessons about not being invincible all over again. I had committed to the fight long before the injury, and it was in one of the largest venues I ever fought in, the Los Angeles Civic Center. Thousands of screaming fans would be there, and my ego wouldn't let me take a bye.

I should have.

Seeing that I had a brace on my knee, my opponent did exactly what any good no-holds-barred fighter should do. He attacked my weakest point, and before I could even land a blow I was incapacitated, flat on the mat, unable to stand. Good old gravity had me down again.

It was humiliating. Worse than my worst nightmare. I struggled out of the cage and hobbled to the locker room, leaning heavily on my corner crew. My career as a fighter ended then and there, all because I couldn't, or wouldn't, recognize that in life, I wasn't the show-runner. Try as I might, I would never be able to bend, or pound, the whole universe to suit my fancy.

So, when the Corvette was taken away from me, maybe I should have taken it as a wakeup call—a signal from the higher powers in the corporation that all was not well with my job—whatever my job was. (Does the fact that I can't even remember what it was give you a clue as to how important it really was?)

But of course I didn't. I just went blithely on my way. It never registered with me that the good times would not keep rolling on autopilot forever. I still thought I was master of my world. Not only was I drawing a nice salary, I'd been given restricted stock options that, at the company's current valuation, were worth a quarter million dollars. Even if my job went away, that was a cushion I could fall back on till I found another job.

This was the summer of 2001, remember. Everybody remembers what happened at the end of that summer. I mean in September.

Oblivious to any problems over the horizon, I kept spending money faster than even my padded salary could keep up with.

But there are people in the world who look for people like me. Because as self-important and all-powerful as we may think we are, they know just how to get us under their thumbs and crush us.

As I ran in Los Angeles' fastest circles, blowing through cash like a Santa Ana wind, there were no doubt many people who saw a target drawn on my back as I hustled past. One of them cozied up to me and became a good friend (I thought). I knew his reputation, and knew that he was the kind of guy with friends who could order a hit that would take you down when you least expected it.

But I'm a tough guy, you know. I figured I could handle him.

There's a TV interview from the late 90s that I have on a DVD. On it you see a TV reporter from a Los Angeles station asking me if I ever get scared going into the cage to fight. I look at him and smile and say "I'm always scared. Yeah, you learn to make fear your friend."

So, it wasn't that this guy didn't scare me. It was just that I figured I could handle him. Fear would be my friend; it would keep me on my toes, and his money would float me through some dry spots until I could collect on the stock options.

It was about this time that I started on a hugely-expensive project that just continued to grow and mushroom completely out of control.

The only thing I have to show for it today is a photocopy of a comic book called *Sheets of Metal,* Issue #1 / Volume #1. Below that on the title page it says "Created by: Nico Hill."

The comic book begins the story of Frank, a ruffian something like me—my alter-ego, I guess—and an amazing 1957 Oldsmobile Delta 88 that comes to him as payment for doing a dirty deed to someone even dirtier than himself. The car is filled with mysteries and special powers that Frank will only gradually come to understand.

I was really into cars, as you know, and sometime that summer I traded the Dragon Wagon to a guy for an old pickup truck that I wanted to restore, plus some cash of course. I'd just gotten a good start on having that truck painted and retooled, when somebody saw it and my dragon motorcycle by the old garage where the truck was being worked on, and made off with both of them. For all I know, they loaded the bike into the back of the truck and drove off in the middle of the night.

That made me really mad, but I'm a fighter. One little setback like that isn't going to stop me in my tracks. I took the insurance money and bought myself—you guessed it—a totally-trashed 1957 Oldsmobile Delta 88.

By then I had a lot of friends in the car-restoration world, and I rallied them all around the project of turning that car into the biggest, baddest beast on the road. I actually named the car The Beast, and had a custom front bumper built for it that was supposed to look like chrome dragon's teeth. Under the hood I put a big block Lincoln engine.

In my mind there was no budget for the project. I mean, no limit on how much I would spend on it.

In the back of my comic book, which was intended to be only the first installment of a long-running serial, we put some information about this actual car around which the story was to circulate. "The car that Frank receives in the story is based on a real life automobile that Nico and a team of over 20 artists and mechanics have brought to life.

... When asked to describe what 'type' of vehicle the car has become thanks to the work that has gone into it and how far from a stock vehicle it has come, Nico replied: 'A Retro Gothic Pro Slam Sled Dragon.' " I'm not even sure what that means, but it sounded pretty awesome to me at the time.

The comic book also tells a little bit about the amazing Nico the Dragon who's behind the project. It shows a picture of me with a couple of belts I'd gotten for risking life and limb in the cage, and it says "Nico officially retired from the ring in the Fall of 2002." (It doesn't mention that I was totally humiliated in front of thousands at the L. A. Civic Center in May of that year.) It then lists my current occupation: "Entrepreneur."

At least that's what I thought I was in 2003 when the book was created.

I had no occupation other than spending money on that car by that time.

But wait a minute. Over 20 artists and mechanics had been employed—over a two-year period—to turn the car into whatever it was supposed to become? If you've ever paid a mechanic to tune up your car, you have some idea how much money I was sinking into this project.

I don't know why I did it.

It was like there was something inside me compelling me, talking to me, urging me to keep going, no matter how much it cost.

I told you about the voices that have spoken to me at various times in my life.

It's been a lifelong journey to learn which voices are safe to listen to.

Some of the money to get the project going came from sources I'm too ashamed to talk about today.

And it was about this time that I got an influx of cash—a loan—from the friend I told you about—the one I was smart enough to be afraid of.

I'd been dumb enough to tell him about the $250,000 in stock options that were just waiting for me to cash in. Because they were restricted, I couldn't sell them before a certain date. When my friend heard that, he decided to cozy up to me even more. "Looks like you could use a little cash to tide you over till the stocks come due," he said one night, that summer of 2001, after we'd had a few drinks.

"Yeah, I'm a little short right now, but you know I got those 250 g's comin' soon."

"What you need's a partner to come in on the business with you," he said.

"What for?" I really knew almost nothing about the business world. But I should have known what it meant when a man with his kinds of affiliations wanted to "partner" with you.

"I mean a partner with some cash to lay out to keep the business running till your ship comes in."

"Yeah, I suppose."

"So, whaddya say I pony up fifty g's or so to tide you over till you can get the money out of the stocks. I'll give you decent rates. You know I will, Nico, man."

It sounded good to me. I couldn't seem to curb my spending, so I was happy to take any loans I could get.

It wasn't long after they took the 'Vette away that they told me they no longer needed my services at the branch of the company I'd transferred to. I was free to go back to the sales desk, or free to walk away.

To go back to the sales desk would be like tapping out in the ring—admitting defeat. Nico wouldn't do that. No way. I'd secretly thumbed my nose at that place when I left, and puffed my chest out. I had proven my worth, and the advancement had been my reward. To go back to sales would be to put the lie to everything I'd told myself about myself! My ego would not allow that.

But the good thing was that enough time had gone by that I could now exercise my stock option.

So I told them they could take a hike with their offer of sending me back to telephone selling, and I took a hike out the door, right down to a brokerage firm to get the money I had coming from the stocks.

There was one minor problem, though.

The company had made the option available to me *as long as I remained an employee of the corporation.* In other words, till about a day ago.

And I'd already spent the $50,000 I'd gotten from my friend with affiliations.

Now was the time to be scared, really scared.

Chapter 4

I've been scared, really scared, many times in my life, almost from the very beginning. But I was taught by my father that to show any sign of fear or pain was to reveal weakness, and real men don't show weakness.

The trouble was that the way he felt he needed to drive that point home to me involved inflicting a lot of pain.

Let me give you a little background on that, because I don't think Dad's original plan for his family was to make my life painful. I think things were pretty much okay when I was small. But as I got a bit bigger, and he grew more frustrated with the turns his life was taking, an incredible amount of rage and violence began to seethe within him, always ready to explode on whatever target was nearest. Unfortunately for me, that was usually me.

At about that same time words began to come into my mind, redemptive words. Words that would eventually change my life and rescue me from the path of perdition I had set myself on, but at the time I couldn't understand what was happening, and neither could anyone else.

To set the stage, I need to tell you that I was baptized into a conservative Christian denomination at the tender age of eight, and it was not long after that that the remarkable gift that would follow me throughout my life was given to me. It was a gift that would try to redeem me over and over again as I bulled my way down a path of suicidal self-destruction.

I honestly don't know how or why I was baptized, and I have no memory of the event. I simply have to believe what I was told about myself by those who were there.

That would include my mother and father, and my brother who is six years younger than I. I'm told that my brother was dedicated to God in that same church at that time, because that denomination does not baptize children until they are old enough to understand the commitment they are making by being baptized.

I don't remember attending church very often as a child, but perhaps my parents had fits and starts of spirituality that occasionally compelled them to drag their kids into religious exercises. My father worked for a company that was run by a church-owned institution, so perhaps it was expected of him that he would "train up his children in the way that they should go" to paraphrase the Bible, and that included having them dedicated and baptized in the church.

I am by nature an extremely rough, violent, and fearless person, and I came by it naturally—genetically—no doubt. And those characteristics were neither drowned nor washed away in the waters of the baptismal tank.

Both my parents had their own backgrounds and heredity to struggle with, and in telling my story the last thing I would want to do is to demonize them and imply that the struggles I went through in life were all their fault. They weren't. I made the decisions that I made, and far too many of them were bad decisions. I alone am to blame for what I suffered and continue to suffer today.

Yes, I continue to suffer today, even though my life has been turned around and I have been sober for nearly four years as I write this. No one can put themselves through the amount of physical abuse that I endured without having residual effects. Headaches, nosebleeds, aching joints, stomach issues, gallstones, you name it, they have not been miraculously lifted from me. Nor have the psychological and social scars that a meth abuser brings upon himself. I say this in part because some may be tempted to think that in telling my story I am somehow glorifying myself or the lifestyle I lived.

Nothing could be farther from the truth.

There is no way you can understand the level of regret that I feel for what I have done to myself. The physical pain I suffer is miserable, but the emotional scars and pain I still bear are what hurt the worst. Parts of my brain have been burned away. Only a miracle could ever restore them, and they are the parts of the brain that make life seem most worthwhile: the parts that allow us to experience pleasure, enjoy a good joke, and enter into meaningful, pleasurable, mutually-satisfying relationships with other human beings.

If I had had a different upbringing, I might have made different choices.

But it is what it is.

The choices we make,

The chances we take,

Often determine our fate.

My father would go to work day by day for a church-owned company, and when he would come home, he all-too-often would begin to hit me, making me the target of unexplained rage. I don't know why he was such an angry man in those days. I do know that his own childhood was difficult, that he was shuttled from family to family with no permanent home, and that when he was 16 his mother and her brother were murdered and my father was the one who found their bodies. I believe those experiences unbalanced him. But many people have difficult childhoods and manage to leave that behind and provide a positive environment for their own children.

Dad, though, seemed to need to use me as the whipping boy for everything bad that had ever happened to him. The idea that he was training me to be tough and endure pain was just his rationalization for what he was doing to me.

Having been raised in that environment, you might understand that I have felt rage myself. I suppose that helps me understand my father better. He is, of course, much older now, and calmer. He seems to have made his peace with the world, and we have reconciled. But in between the time when I lived with him and today, he spent years living as what is known as a one-percent biker—a member of one of the motorcycle gangs that wear their outlaw status and contempt for society's restraints as a badge of honor.

But the fact that Dad took out his frustrations on someone smaller and weaker than himself did something to me. Even in my darkest hours, I always wanted to protect children from abuse by adults. And because he was emotionally abusive to my mother too, I always tried to be a protector for women as well.

My mother was a strong person in many ways, and nobody, not even my father, was allowed to walk over her. Her way of defending herself was with words, so the house where I lived as a young boy was often filled with shouts, screams, swearing, threats, and imprecations.

I would retreat to my room, cover my head with my pillow, and wish that it all would end.

But then mysterious words began to swirl through my mind. Words and thoughts that you would not expect to occur to an eight-year-old.

One time, after a particularly loud parental altercation, my mother came to my room, tears streaming down her face.

"How are you doing, son?" she asked.

I didn't respond.

"Did you—I mean, how much of—did you hear what your father accused me of?"

She was stammering around, trying to find a way to make sure I would take her side. I was always getting caught in the middle of these fights, both parents trying to make me see things their way.

I still didn't respond to her. I was sick of being used as a pawn in the power plays that raged around me.

"Is there something you want to tell me, Nicholas?"

I just stared.

"Say something, Nicholas! I'm your mother, don't just

gawk at me like you don't know who I am!" She sounded desperate.

That's when the words came out. Words I'd never heard before, but they somehow flowed from my mouth as though I'd been rehearsing them all my life.

Life is a game, winners and losers, preachers and boozers.
If you ask me, it's all the same
And no one gives you nothin'
you must try and try again
Even though it's often to the bitter end

And is there a moral to this story
You mean after all this, can't you feel the glory?
Is there a silver lining around that cloud,
Or do we go through life with our heads bowed?

The dreams we have, they stay inside
The people with the power keeping our hands tied.

My mother's mouth hung open for what seemed like several minutes. Finally she collected herself enough to begin to quiz me. "Where did you hear that?"

I shrugged.

"How did you memorize it?"

I shrugged again.

"Where is it written down? I want to see it."

"It's not."

"What do you mean it's not? You had to read it somewhere."

"No I didn't. I made it up."

She just stared, then turned around and left my room, closing the door behind her. She never asked me about the words or mentioned them to me again, ever, for the rest of her life.

I had no idea where the words had come from, and probably had very little conception of what they meant.

But they stuck with me. I can still recite them at will forty-five years later. And I have a much better idea of what they mean today.

I wish I had had a better understanding of their lesson back in 2001, when my friend with affiliations offered to loan me $50,000. The loan gave him power over me—power that could tie my hands. But it would take a lifelong journey before I came to anything but a nominal understanding of the gift that was given to me that night. I'm sure I don't fully understand it, or its purpose, yet. I expect to be discovering new facets for all of the rest of my journey.

I wish I could tell you that the minor miracle that occurred in my bedroom began a process of change that made everything better in our home. But our life wasn't like an episode of *The Waltons*. Miraculous messages and inspired insights didn't instantly transform us into a family who sweetly called "Good Night" to each other every night as the lights were shut off one by one to the accompaniment of guitar, zither, and trumpet.

The beatings continued, and my father continued to challenge me to man-up and take it without a whimper. But every time I got a little braver and held the tears and screams back a little longer, he would up the ante by pommeling me longer and harder.

Then he got me started in martial-arts training so I'd be able to defend myself—from others, of course, not from him. I didn't dare raise a hand against him.

Finally the animosity between my parents grew to the point where they divorced and my brother and I went to live with our mother.

Our visits with my father after that were sporadic as his life descended into more and more decadence and violence. My next major memory comes from a time a few years later. I think I was eleven at the time. My brother and I had been sent to spend a few days living with our father and a woman he planned to marry. But soon after we arrived, my dad walked out the door, leaving us in Francine's care. He didn't come home that night or the next, and by the third day Francine was very drunk and very angry.

She staggered from the kitchen into the living room where I was watching TV. My brother had already fallen asleep and been put to bed. "Where's your father?" her words were slurred.

I looked up from the program I was watching and said, "I don't know."

"Yes you do. You know where he is, and what he's doing."

"No I don't."

"Yes you do!" She flopped on the couch, leaning back against the arm. She was wearing only a man's dress shirt and underwear, and she made no attempt to be modest. "Why won't you tell me where he is?" she whined. "Just tell me. I won't tell on you."

I didn't look at her or answer.

"Tell me!" she demanded, leaning forward and glaring at me. "Tell me where he is, and what he's doing!"

"How should I know?" I still didn't look at her.

"You know! Why won't you tell me?"

When I ignored her, she tried tears on me. "Why won't you tell me?" she sobbed. But I really had no concern for the woman, so I just tried to tune her out.

Seeing that her strategy wasn't working, she struggled to her feet and came over to me and grabbed me by the arm. "You hungry?" she asked. "Want something to drink?"

"No, I'm okay."

"Come on," she said, tugging on my arm.

I tried to resist, but she wouldn't let go, so I stood up and she led me to the kitchen. "Just look at that!" she said, waving her arm over food that she had set out for a meal two days earlier. "It's all spoiled. Rotten. Dirty. Rotten. Awful. And it's all your father's fault. Where is he?"

"I don't know!" I said angrily. "Now leave me alone!"

I could easily have hurt her, made her let me go, but somewhere along the line I had resolved never to strike a woman, so I just took it.

She dragged me to the table then, and picked up the whiskey bottle she'd been drinking from. "Want some?" she swayed as she offered it to me.

"No!"

"Look at this," she said, waving her arm over the table again.

I took a closer look at the table and saw that she had spread some very explicit pornographic pictures there. "Just look at that," she broke down in tears and flopped into a chair and laid her head on her arms on the table, sobbing.

I didn't know what to do.

I turned around and started to go back to the living room, but she jumped up and seized me by the shoulders and turned me around to face her, a leering smile on her face. "Come with me," she said, and took me by the hand and led me to my father's bedroom.

My mind has blocked out memories of exactly what happened next.

I had just entered puberty, and she apparently thought she was Mrs. Robinson.

Whatever happened, it was traumatic enough that my mind mercifully refuses to reconstruct it. All I remember is that when it was over, I was horrified and got up and headed for the door. "No! Don't go! Stay with me," she pled.

I didn't answer, so she started crying.

While she wasn't watching, I stole money from her purse. When she'd cried herself to sleep, I went to the room where my brother was sleeping and woke him up. "Come on, we've got to leave," I said. He was only five or six at the time, but he did as I said, and we went out the door, found a bus stop, and somehow, using the money I'd stolen, I took us on a series of busses till we arrived home about thirty miles away.

It is hard for me, to this day, to explain the full impact that that encounter with Francine had on me. The specific events that followed seem to be blocked from my memory, just as the event itself is.

I know I felt ashamed, dirty. I didn't understand what had happened, but I knew two things for sure: 1. There were no adults in my life that I could trust. 2. I was angry—no, make that enraged.

When my brother and I got home, there was another incident. At the time my mother had a live-in boyfriend—she called him her fiancé, but I don't know if they had actually set a wedding date or not.

Mom had a hard time making good choices in life. Especially when it came to men.

The guy who was living with her at the time wasn't any better to her than my dad had been. They were constantly having arguments and physical confrontations. When my brother and I got home, this guy was lounging around the apartment in a stained wife-beater t-shirt and boxers.

I was only eleven, but pretty big for my age, and I had years of martial-arts training behind me. Stressed as I was by what I'd just been put through, I must have walked up to him, glared in his eyes, and told him to get out. When he didn't respond, I think I put my fist through the wall, or my foot through a patio door, I'm not sure what. Whatever it was, it scared him enough that he packed up and left, never to return.

When Mom came home from work later that day, she asked where he was, and I just told her he left. She didn't say any more about it, didn't ask why Danny and I came back early. I'm sure I had some explaining to do about the damage I'd done in my rage, but that's about all.

I was never able to tell any adults about what Francine had done.

I didn't trust any of them.

From that day forward I kept my thoughts, my emotions, my fears, my hopes all to myself. I was the only person I trusted with them. I became the model of total self-reliance, not letting anyone see inside of me.

Because I'd learned that I couldn't trust the authority figures in my life who should have had my back, I missed out on learning to truly trust anyone or anything. I withdrew within myself, and seemed unable to realize that even an island is subject to the larger forces of wind, wave, and tide that surround it.

There were forces that were chipping away at me all through those years, wearing me down to my rock-hard, unfeeling skeleton. By the mid-2000s I wanted them to finish the job and take me away from all the pain I'd stored up inside.

But in 2001, when my stock options were taken away, and I found myself in debt for 50 g's to a group of people even bigger and badder than me, I thought I had to solve the problem all by myself.

Chapter 5

My world had collapsed around me.

The world I'd thought I had on a string.

I had gotten the string tangled, and now the world I thought of as my yo-yo wouldn't come back to me.

Worse yet, it seemed that I was now the one dangling—on the end of somebody else's string.

I went to the friend who had invested $50,000 in me, with the understanding that he would get it all back as soon as I cashed in my stock option, and explained to him what the broker had told me: My option had evaporated the minute I was taken off the company payroll, and I didn't have his money and didn't see how I was going to get it.

He was very calm about it, in the way that a person can be calm when they know they are in a position of power and have the situation under control. "So, what are we going to do?" he asked.

"I'll get the money for you," I said.

"We can take care of those people if you want us to."

"No, no. I got it man."

"You sure?"

"'Course I am!" I think I pulled off a confident smile.

"We're good, then?"

"Don't trip. I got your back!"

He grabbed my hand to shake it, and held on, tilting his head, trying to peer through the mask of concealed emotions I'd worn all my life, but he'd have needed

Superman eyes to see what was really going on in my brain. "Handle it."

"You got it."

I squeezed his hand hard, then turned to go. I hadn't let him see me sweat, but I knew what I had to do next was pretty risky. "Make fear your friend," I reminded myself.

The next morning I donned a business suit and walked into the building where I'd worked for so many years and went right past the reception and security areas like it was just another day at the office. In the elevator I nonchalantly pressed the button for the Penthouse where Stewart, the CEO's, suite was.

Stewart's assistant tried to stop me from barging into his office, but I just flashed her a friendly smile and went right on in.

Stewart was on the phone, his back to the door, looking out over the San Fernando Valley through his floor-to-ceiling window on the world. Out of the corner of my eye I caught a glimpse of one of the burly guys he'd started to surround himself with in the recent weeks since he'd started handing out pink slips to once-powerful players at the office. I glanced around at the man by the door, just long enough to confirm that he had a bulge on the left side of his chest. Probably a 9 mm. Sig Sauer, locked and loaded, I guessed.

Hearing me come in, Stewart rotated enough my way to see who was violating his private space unannounced. He shot a glance at the man by the door, who started to move toward me, but Stewart shook his head, and the man moved back.

Stewart calmly finished his conversation, then swung around and hung up the phone. "Nick, what can I do for you?" He looked at me, then to his bodyguard, then back to me.

I followed his eyes to the big man by the door and looked right at the bulge on his chest. "You got a weapon, but you got to reach for it. I *am* a weapon," I said. "But I'm not here to hurt no one."

I turned back to Stewart. "I just need to share a little information with you Stewart, then I'll be outa your hair for good."

"Information about what, Nick?" Stewart picked up a fountain pen he'd laid on his desk and returned it to its holder.

"About my stock option."

"What about it?"

"They won't let me exercise it down at the brokerage."

"Of course they won't. You don't work here anymore. There were contingencies on that option. You should have read the fine print, Nick."

I seldom even read the bold print on papers I was asked to sign, and Stewart probably knew that.

"We've got a problem, then."

"I don't have a problem, Nick. I can imagine maybe that's a problem for you. But *we* don't have a problem."

"Yes we do," I said, glancing over my shoulder at the bodyguard as I moved right up to the front of Stewart's desk and sat down without waiting for his invitation.

I didn't need to watch what the big guy behind me was doing, I could read it in Stewart's eyes as he set his lips in a straight line and shook his head at his man again.

"What sort of a problem do *we* have, Nick?"

I explained to him that a friend of mine had put up $50,000 toward my new business venture, secured by my stock option.

"I'm not following you, Nick. I still don't see how that is *our* problem. That's *your* problem. Just give him his fifty grand back, and the problem's solved."

"I don't have it."

"What did you do with fifty thousand dollars, Nick? You can't have spent it all already. ... Can you?"

"I gave it to my brother to make a down payment on a house." That was a total fabrication. Like all the other money that had slipped through my fingers, I could no more account for where those dollars had gone than I could count the grains of sand on Venice Beach.

"You took money the mob gave you for a business venture and handed it to your brother?" He'd been around me enough to know better than to be surprised at almost any stupid thing I might do, but I think that genuinely shocked him. My friend wasn't actually Mafia-connected, but I didn't mind if Stewart assumed that he was.

I nodded.

"I wouldn't want to be in your shoes, Nick. I mean, I feel really, really bad for you. But that's your mistake, your loss. What do you want me to do about it?"

"Well, here's the thing," I said, leaning in real close to him and speaking very softly. "You see, I'm protecting you right now."

"From what?"

"For me to know and you to find out," I said. "I'm not throwing anybody under the bus. In my world, snitches wear stitches, so let me put it to you this way, Stewart." I leaned a little closer and spoke very quietly. "You're on the train tracks, you just don't hear the whistle blowing."

He swallowed hard and sat back in his chair. I could see sweat glistening in the webs of his fingers. He looked up at his bodyguard. "Give us a few minutes, Serge."

Serge was looking at me, not him. "You sure about that, boss?"

"Nick and I go back a long ways. You wouldn't want to hurt anyone here, would you Nick?"

"I think we can work something out," I said. I still considered Stewart to be my friend.

"We'll be okay Serge." He motioned with his eyes toward the door. Serge's eyes gave me a meaningful once-over, then he turned and went out.

"I could probably cut you a check for five grand, you know, maybe once a month out of petty cash," Stewart offered.

"That's not gonna cut it," I said. "You got any idea what the interest rate is these guys want?"

"That's about the best I can do."

"No, here's what you're going to do," I said. I pulled out

my wallet and produced a scrap of paper with two bank account numbers written on it. "I really don't want to hurt anybody, so here's what's going to happen. Tomorrow morning at the crack of dawn, $50,000 is going to show up in this account. I put my finger on the first number on the scrap. And $5,000 is going to show up in this account— that's for me, for my trouble."

"I can't just..."

The way I shrugged my shoulders and put my hands palm up stopped him.

"Nick, it's not that easy."

"Listen, I don't want to hurt anyone, man. You know me. But some people in this office building are going to start feeling some significant pain real soon if you can't work this out. You know who I am. You know what I can do."

"Nick, be reasonable, buddy. I'll see what I can do, okay?" He almost choked on his words.

"Give me your word."

"Sure, of course."

"Good. 'Cause if you're not good on it, it's not going to be me you're dealing with. You understand that, right?"

"Right."

"Good, man!" I gave him a big smile as I stood up. "Well, it's been really nice chatting with you."

"Yeah, right," he said absently, standing with me. I reached across the desk and shook his hand. With my left hand I pushed the scrap with the accounts on it closer. When I released his hand, I looked down at it, then looked up at him and winked.

Playing the enforcer like that didn't come naturally to me. I was usually the guy with the quick smile and a ready joke to put people at ease. But if you look through my movie credits, you'll notice that sometimes I'm simply listed as Thug Number Three or something like that. If Stewart made good on his promise, it would pay for all those acting lessons.

Chapter 6

I left the building hating what I'd just done. Hating myself because I'd had to do it.

Sure, I could play the role of the tough, confident guy who would always get his way one way or the other. But in reality nothing was going my way. My life was spinning completely out of control, and only the carefully-practiced façade I wore kept anybody else from recognizing how little confidence I really had.

I breathed a sigh of amazed relief the next morning when I checked the accounts. The money was there! All of it! Including the $5,000 fee I'd exacted for making the deal happen. And Stewart even did me better than I had asked. He deposited $5,000 each month for six months as severance pay!

I gave my friend with affiliations the $50,000, and he soon disappeared from my life. But I kept on going through money faster than it was coming in.

Worse than my financial condition, though, was my mental, spiritual, and emotional state.

I had just lost the best, most-stable, longest-lasting job I had ever had. Worse yet I had burned my bridges. I had seriously considered going to my immediate boss back on the sales floor, who had become a close friend, and asking for my old job back. That wasn't going to happen now, after I'd just extorted over fifty grand out of the CEO.

Fortunately I had recently started working in movies

again, and that brought some nice pay checks, but it wasn't steady work.

There were also the fights.

It was probably good that I had those. Most of them were just small, local things, held at somebody's gym, or in a parking lot somewhere. The amount of money I got for risking my life in those cages was slim compensation for the risks I was taking. I'd turned 40 that year, and I was going up against guys a lot younger than me. Old injuries were starting to take their toll, but I still managed to keep my win-loss ratio high enough to be of interest to promoters who loved profiting off other people's pain.

The fighting life is almost as much about image, publicity, and posturing as it is about pugilistic prowess. Don't get me wrong—if you haven't trained faithfully in some form of martial arts, and you aren't in peak physical condition, there's no way you'd last more than a few seconds up against any of the men I fought. They are really tough guys, really big guys, really strong guys. They've all studied and practiced the art of inflicting maximum pain with minimum effort; they've learned to endure a lot of pain themselves, and they don't care how bad they have to hurt you to get you to the point where you'll tap out.

I wouldn't have gotten any fights in those days, if I hadn't projected an image that made fans think of me as something a lot bigger than I ever felt in real life. To them I was this handsome hulk of a movie star who didn't just play a tough guy on the big screen, I really was a tough guy who could hold his own, caged like a tiger, fighting for my life against some really scary people.

I guess I actually believed my own press releases, as they say, at least for a time. I thought of myself as a really cool guy, and played the role, continuing to bar hop all over Hollywood, picking up, and taking advantage of, every pretty girl that my image could attract.

I still looked tough on the outside. But on the inside I was crumbling, barely able to hold it together, pouring what money I didn't squander on my social life into The Beast—

the '57 Olds that was slowly taking shape, preparing for its debut when Nico the Dragon would come roaring up the Boulevard in the most awesome Retro Gothic Pro Slam Sled that Tinsel Town would ever see.

In Hollywood everything is about image, and I was going to project an image that would attract a lot of attention. Not only would the car be awesome, it—along with my alter ego Frank—would be the main character in a brand new comic book series. Blockbuster movie deals with me as the lead couldn't be far down the pike, could they? I didn't think so, especially after I attended Comic-Con in 2003 and met with some pretty impressive studio contacts.

The car, and the comics, became my life, the only things that were holding me together while I was falling apart in other ways.

Up to this point I had never used hard drugs, other than maybe a few brief experiments. I hated the very idea of drug use—despised what I had seen it do to other people.

I could trace my hatred of drugs back to my childhood.

My younger brother was born with several handicaps, which I believe was one of the things that contributed to the rage my father poured out against my mother and me. When Mom and Dad would be screaming invectives back and forth across the kitchen, my dad would often cast the blame for Danny's problems on Mom, because for years she had taken a shopping-list of prescription and over-the-counter drugs on a daily basis.

That planted the idea in my mind that taking drugs was a bad thing. Then, after my parents separated, they got back together again for a couple of years and started taking in foster kids. The amazing thing to me is that despite how hard my dad was on me, and despite the constant arguing and fighting, to the public my parents projected an image that won them recognition as role models. Twice they were named foster-parents-of-the-year for Los Angeles County!

I think I was only in fourth or fifth grade when one of the foster kids, a girl about seventeen I think, tried to kill herself with an overdose. The image of the paramedics coming and putting IVs in her arm, taking her away on a gurney, burned itself into my mind, and I promised myself that I would never do drugs.

With the exception of alcohol, it was a promise I pretty well kept for thirty years. Booze was my only go-to drug to try to soothe the mental and physical pain I was enduring.

But after I lost my big cash-cow job and had my stock options ripped away with it, something changed in my mind, and I set out on a path of self-loathing and self-destruction that ten years later had turned me into a skeleton of a man who looked forward to nothing more than dying and ending his pain.

That morning when I threatened to cause people pain around my former office, I knew I was capable of doing exactly that—although I didn't really intend to.

The amount of rage and just plain physical meanness that could pump its way through my body and out through my fists, elbows, knees, and feet was legendary—at least in my own mind and in fight-promoters' handbills.

I knew I was capable of really hurting people. It was what I got paid to do.

But any responsible sensei who teaches martial arts also instills in his students the importance of self-control. He or she may turn you into a lethal weapon, capable of killing a person with your bare hands, but along with that you'll get instruction in meditation and other mental/spiritual exercises that will enable you to harness your new-found powers and release them only when needed.

I was a sensei myself. For many years my friend Shark and I operated a small by-invitation-only dojo in a side room of a gym owned by another close friend. It was called Strategic Street Self-Defense, and our students included police officers, bouncers, and sometimes tiny little women who we taught how to ward off attackers with non-lethal moves.

As a responsible sensei, I drilled into every student that what they were learning was not to be used for getting even.

They studied under me to learn how to defend themselves, not how to attack their enemies.

As I glared into Stewart's eyes that morning, I was fighting back the urge to hurt everyone who had done me wrong.

On some level I would have enjoyed going through the halls, office to office, pulling one paunchy executive after another up from his padded leather chair and breaking some bones in his face, but at the same time I would have known I was violating my own code of ethics, and I didn't want to do that.

Fortunately I didn't have to.

But when I strode out of the building, hoping Stewart would make good on his promise, all the adrenalin that had built up during our confrontation was still circulating through my veins.

I wanted to hurt somebody, and after I'd had a few drinks, a weird logic took hold of me. Rather than hurting the people who had made me angry, I would take out my rage on myself. I would hurt myself, destroy myself, not others.

I didn't instantly decide to start snorting crystal meth to hurt myself. No, drugs were still abhorrent to me. It would take a few more twists to wrap my mind around the idea of using the only thing I hated more than myself to kill myself.

But once I got that idea in my head, nothing short of a miracle would take it out.

Chapter 7

Getting things in exact chronological order, with the proper dates attached, is certainly not one of my talents. All I can do is tell you what happened, and about when I think it happened. I'll try to keep things in the right sequential order when I tell you about them, because one thing did lead to another, and speaking of leading, I know now that all the while I thought I was running my own show, I was actually being led by unseen influences.

There's a saying that you'll often hear me repeat these days, as I reflect on the path my life has taken: "Satan builds you up in order to tear you down, but God tears you down in order to build you up."

Looking back on the time when I lost my job in 2001, and what I did in the aftermath, I can see that pattern playing out.

I had come into some money in a way that wasn't strictly above board. I had about $100,000 in the bank, and if I had invested it wisely or used it to get some training in a profession, my life might have turned out differently. I might not have had to descend into the depths of hell before I could begin to look up and get things back in order.

But as soon as I started the project I called "The Beast," the 1957 Oldsmobile I was having restored, it was as though an unseen power took control of me, and nothing could stop my obsession with turning that car into the most awesome street machine in L. A.

My plan was to exalt myself as the owner of The Beast.

In reality The Beast was taking possession of my life.

I was swiftly draining my bank account, but I would spare no expense.

I spent all my days and many of my nights at the shop, supervising every detail of the work being done.

The people there amazed me. They could pull 20-hour days one right after another, and always seemed energetic and enthusiastic.

I figured it was the drugs they were using, but the hatred I'd developed as a child for what drugs did to people kept me from wanting any part of that.

Then, about the end of the year, I was on my way to a Christmas party—one of those famous, sodden bashes that Hollywood is known for. The host was a good friend of mine who owned a popular strip club, so there would be plenty of eye candy to pick from.

You may think it is demeaning for me to speak of the young, beautiful women who attended these parties as "eye candy," but that was how I thought of them in those days. And as far as I could tell, they enjoyed playing that role, as long as it got the attention of men who would treat them decently and spend a lot of money on them.

I always tried to treat them decently, and of course money was not an issue. I'm not excusing my lifestyle, just sharing how I thought about it at the time. Today I can see how wrong it was, and how it was leading me on a downhill path. But at the time I thought I was near the top of the world and still climbing.

It was a cold night by Los Angeles standards, with a smattering of rain in the forecast, but for some reason some of my buds and I decided it would be sweet to roar up to the party on our Harleys.

The spits and spats of rain that hit the streets that night were just enough to make them slick, and for the first time in decades of charging about on a thunder horse, I went into a corner skid that I couldn't control and ended up sliding across the pavement on my rear, ripping my pants, but fortunately not getting hurt beyond a few bruises. I picked myself up and we went on to the party.

The eye candy I picked up that night was a stripper who actually went by the name Candy. We talked, exchanged numbers, and I filed her away as a good candidate for a night on the town.

A month or two later I decided to find out if she'd really given me her number, and when she picked up, she said she remembered me. We set a date and headed for Hollywood.

My way of making an impression on a girl in those days was to go club-hopping. Primo Hollywood night life always centers around a few exclusive spots. Whatever destination is at the top of the heap in any given season is almost impossible to get into unless you've got connections, or are on the industry's current A-list (think Russell Crowe or Sandra Bullock).

I never made the A-list, but I did make a lot of connections, partly because I'd worked as a bouncer in a lot of different places, and done security for some pretty important people. So, it was easy for me to make a big impression on Candy by taking her from club to club, being received with open arms everywhere.

The problem with that was that I always showed my appreciation by ordering drinks. By the end of the night I was anything but at the top of my game. By time we got back to Candy's place, I was having strong regrets about how much I'd consumed. At least we'd had the good sense to go by limo that night instead of driving!

She invited me in, but I said No thanks—I think I'd better get home. My place was just a few blocks away, and I figured I'd walk. The fresh air would do me good.

"Aw, come on in, just for a minute. I've got something that'll help you feel better."

I'd say that it was against my better judgment that I accepted her invitation, but that wouldn't really be true. I had so much alcohol in my system by then that my better judgment was completely anesthetized—out cold and down for the count, unable to raise its bothersome head or wave a red flag to stop me from making a terrible mistake.

I didn't realize I had an alcohol addiction at the time. I told myself I had it all under control, but recently a close friend who was listening to me tell about something from my past stopped me and said, "You're an alcoholic."

"No I'm not."

"Then how come all your stories about your past involve drinking?"

As I thought more about it, I had to admit to myself that alcohol had taken over my life by then—a bad situation that was about to lead me into something even worse.

With my better judgment K. O.'d, I entered Candy's house, and her world. "I'm a white witch," she told me. "I use my powers only for good."

All I could do as I sat on her couch was hang my head and nod slightly. Any more movement would have sent the contents of my stomach erupting onto her carpet.

"I can work a spell that will take all your pain away," she offered.

What did I have to lose? I was so sick and drunk I wasn't sure I could even make it as far as my apartment just a couple of blocks away.

She went into her bathroom, and when she came out a couple minutes later, she said she had a little present for me "in there."

I staggered to my feet and wobbled my way to where she stood, looking into the little room. On the counter beside the sink was a thick, bumpy line of white crystals.

"That's your spell?" I said, trying to focus my eyes.

"It will take all the pain away."

"Nah, I don't do drugs. I may drink like a fish, and I've smoked some weed. But no hard drugs. Not for me."

"Just try it once. You don't know what you're missing."

"It won't do anything for me." I have no idea where that stupid idea came from. Maybe I thought I was such a macho man that no drug could touch me. More likely I was just too drunk to think at all.

"We'll see about that," she smiled seductively. "Go on. There's a razor there—you got to break up the crystals first."

"I know, I know." I'd seen the movie *Scarface,* so I figured I knew how to prep and snort drugs without some white witch tutoring me.

I stumbled into the bathroom, and with Al Pacino as my instructor, I prepped the meth crystals, then put a straw in my nose and inhaled hard and fast.

I stood there, staring at her for a moment, not feeling a thing. "See, I told you it wouldn't affect me!" I gloated—but only for a few seconds. Then it hit me and my world started to spin.

"Just lie down for a minute, sweetie," she said as she helped me find my way back to the sofa.

I flopped onto the soft cushions and put my legs up on the armrest, and that's when the full effects hit me.

Joy flooded my brain.

My nausea evaporated.

My arms and legs that had taken so many hard blows from martial artists of all types ceased to hurt.

I thought I had died and gone to heaven.

When you're on the wrong path, everything begins to look right.

So even though I had just taken the first step on the road to a personal hell where I would be tormented for the next ten years, I thought I was in heaven.

Everything was fine.

Everything looked beautiful.

Candy, who was a real head-turner to start with, looked a hundred times better to me.

I think I know now how Eve felt after she took the first bite of the forbidden fruit.

I had found my poison—or it had found me.

He will lead you to your poison well.
If you thirst, he will feed you your drink.

But if you dare sip from that cup,
You will never again rest or be at peace.

I had at last found the thing my soul had been craving—
I thought.

I won't lie to you. That first experience with meth
delivered on its promise. It triggered neurons in the precise
part of my brain that the Creator has placed there in order
to allow us to experience all the positive human emotions—
joy, peace, laughter, closeness, flooding the pleasure
centers of my nervous system with chemicals that the body
manufactures in limited amounts.

Yes, the drugs brought an amazing sense of pleasure.

But the trouble is that using drugs to stimulate those
parts of the brain over and over again eventually wears
them out, just like any other part of the body that gets
overused.

To this day I suffer the consequences of the years of
overstimulation that followed. I pray to God that someday
my ability to sense pleasure without having to resort to
illicit drugs may return. But the scars on my brain, along
with many other scars from years of rough living, may stay
with me for the rest of my life.

The thought of falling back into addiction frightens me
terribly. Once you first cross that threshold and begin to
rely on drugs to soothe your aches and provide you with
joy, the temptation to return to their alluring charms will
follow you for the rest of your life.

Even now the struggle to resist the appeal of meth's
instant gratification is a day-by-day battle for me. I wish I
had never taken that first step, and whenever I get a
chance, I plead with young people not to make the mistakes
I did. *Rock bottom starts the day you got 'em* I say.

Chapter 8

That first taste of crystal meth in 2002 didn't instantly lead to disaster.

I managed to hold myself somewhat together for several more years, just using drugs occasionally. If you Google me on the Internet, or visit my web page, you can see evidence that up to about 2005, I was still a fairly functional member of society.

In 2002 I retired from the MMA fight circuit after a humiliating defeat in front of a large crowd at the Los Angeles Civic Center. I told you before about how I hurt my knee by making a small misstep on the set of a movie. That happened not long before that big fight, and to make matters worse, as I walked into the arena for that fight, wearing a brace on my leg, one of my corner men, Matt Burch, lost his balance and his weight came onto me as he tried to keep from falling. (You might have seen Matt on the reality show *Operation Repo*. He's the burly, bald costar.) My knee gave off a sickening pop as Matt's weight came onto me. I never should have gone into the ring, but I did anyway, and my opponent attacked that knee, injuring it even worse and ending my fighting career.

After that disastrous fight I turned my full attention to my '57 Olds, "The Beast," and the comic book or graphic novel called *Sheets of Metal*. I began pouring myself and all the money I had left into creating a true monster car.

While that may seem like a really bad idea in retrospect,

at the time it seemed to have great potential. An article in the August, 2003 issue of *Tailgate Magazine* featured me and several of my projects, including The Beast, and that garnered me a lot of attention. When I attended the Comic-Con in San Diego in 2003, I met some pretty powerful people who were interested in developing the comic book series, and even started talking about building a movie franchise around it. But for one reason or another none of those ideas ever panned out.

The car itself looked fabulous when all the work on it was done.

Unfortunately it turned out to be a bit of a metaphor for my own life at that point.

I still looked good on the outside, and could put on a good show, but deep inside there was something major wrong with me. I was depending more and more on meth to give me the energy to get through the day. I was turbocharging my life, but headed for a meltdown.

When the car was pulled out of the shop, it looked fantastic. It even drove good for a few miles. But when the guy who took it out for a test run revved the engine, all hell broke loose—literally. Pistons exploded through the top of the engine block! Somebody had failed to install some part right, and the turbocharged engine with huge chrome huffers mounted on the hood tore itself to pieces on the spot. I never even got to drive it.

It was indeed a metaphor for what was going on in my life.

In 2004 I was hired by a producer at the Spike TV Network to play host on my own TV reality show called *Boom!* It was a fun show to work on—as one friend described it, it was kind of *MythBusters* on Meth. Not that we used drugs on the show or anything like that, but one of the things that keeps fans coming back for more *MythBusters* is the explosions and car wrecks that Adam, Jamie, Kari, Grant, and Tory manage to work into almost every episode.

Boom! was all about the explosions.

In short I got paid to blow stuff up and destroy it in other ways too.

It was great fun, and for a year brought in a weekly paycheck even bigger than I was getting before I lost my other job. If you see me in those shows, I look like a pretty happy, together guy, having a lot of fun without the aid of ingested chemicals. The drugs and demons hadn't fully taken over my life—yet.

Unfortunately *Boom!* was a flash in the pan. We filmed a dozen episodes, but then some change in management led to the show being cancelled even before all of them aired.

About the same time when I was doing *Boom!* I also got one of my biggest movie roles in *No Rules,* which was written and directed by Pamela Anderson's brother Gerry. Pamela had a part in the movie, as did other well-known actors including Tom Sizemore, Gary Busey, my friend "Shark," and Randy Couture

I hadn't exactly made Hollywood's A-list, but I felt like I was getting close. The buzz around *No Rules* was so positive that we were on track for making a sequel.

Then something went wrong, and the movie didn't even get a theatrical release. I think it finally came out as a video around the end of 2004.

The cancellation of my TV show, along with the failure of *No Rules*, and the explosion of The Beast's engine, added to all the aches and pains I was suffering from injuries, sent me into a tailspin.

Life had been cruel to me, I thought.

Everyone and everything seemed to have conspired against me.

I was angry and looking for revenge.

But back when I was fired and robbed of my stock options in 2001, I had decided that I wasn't going to take out my anger on others. And now my resolve to take it out on myself surfaced again

I began to pursue self-destruction in earnest.

Chapter 9

The next five years of my life are a fog, a wasteland of blurry images that I have no desire to see clearly.

If I were to tell you the names of some of the people I was involved with in those dark times, you could look them up on the Internet and see hundreds of pictures of the type of debauchery I descended into in my attempt to obliterate myself. I know this only because close friends have done the research and found these images, including one picture of me in a drug-induced haze, looking more dead than alive.

I won't go there myself. I do not have a computer now, and I don't want to have one. I wouldn't trust myself with one.

If you have never struggled to overcome an addiction, you probably can't understand how dangerous it would be for me, even after several years of sobriety, to revisit those times and places in my mind. Seeing the images on a computer screen could trigger thoughts and desires that I never want to take control of me again.

I hope you will understand if we pass quickly over that part of my life.

There would be nothing helpful or redemptive about going into detail about the kinds of places I lived or the things I did, even if I could remember them.

In one sense those are lost years—lost to me as far as accomplishing anything worthwhile, and thankfully for the most part lost to my memory.

But here's the great thing about redemption: God can take even the garbage in our lives and use it to build something good. He's doing that for me now—but only because I survived. Most people who take the path that I did are not so lucky—or so blessed. You can see them on city sidewalks most anywhere, living in cardboard boxes covered by scraps of plastic, garbage bags and the like, trying to stay out of the elements, staring at the world through glassy eyes, muttering curses at passersby from nearly toothless mouths, so ashamed of what they have become that they heap their self-loathing on strangers. And those are just the ones who haven't killed themselves yet with an overdose or some disease they picked up on the street.

That could have been me.

Fortunately I never ended up living on the street, but I easily could have.

By the time I began my quest for self-destruction in earnest, I had learned a lot about the drug culture—especially about users and suppliers of crystal meth, and I knew how to find them.

There's a tabloid newspaper in Los Angeles that caters to the drug culture. All I had to do was search the ads at the back, looking for certain code words that are associated with various types of drugs.

I first made contact with the woman I will refer to as Dee (for Dominatrix—which was just one of many roles she played) through one of those ads.

I wasn't looking for a serious, long-lasting involvement in her world, so when I first went to meet her, I took a taxi and used a false name to keep her from finding out anything about me.

She met me at the door of her apartment, scantily clad and half out of her mind. Once inside I was taken to a large, dark room with computer screens and televisions scattered about, all showing triple-x rated pornography. Several people were there with her, all of them high on something.

I wasn't interested in the porn, and felt no sexual attraction to Dee. I was there for the drugs, and I soon learned that she had plenty.

I showed her a small bag I'd brought with me that had about two grams of crystal meth.

She just smiled. "So you think that's a good amount do you?" She went into a side room and brought out a bag that had probably seven or eight ounces of pure crystal.

She put the bag on a table and took out two large crystals and put them into a bong—a pipe with liquid in it to cool the fumes that would be created when she put it over a flame. She then heated the crystals and inhaled and blew a cloud out in my face.

I was mesmerized! That looked amazing to me. Wow! They call me the dragon—but I'd never breathed fire like that!

"You ready?" she asked.

I nodded, and she handed the bong to me along with a cigarette lighter. I wanted to act like I knew what I was doing, but I was already high from snorting meth, and my hands shook, tilting the bong so the water from the reservoir spilled down onto the crystals—a disaster in the eyes of anyone who knew what I was supposed to do.

"You idiot!" she screamed at me. "I thought you knew what you were doing," and she brought her arm around, trying to backhand slap me. My fighter's instincts kicked in, and I blocked her blow, then looked at the pipe in my hands and tilted it up to my lips and drank the liquid.

Her fiery eyes went wide and her face went pale. When I didn't immediately choke or collapse on the floor in cardiac arrest, she said, "Oh, you are crazy, aren't you?"

I have no idea how long I stayed on that first visit, perhaps a whole day, maybe a night as well. We sat around doing drugs and talking—weird talk, esoteric stuff that I'm sure wouldn't sound the least bit intelligent to anyone without chemicals in their system, but it all seemed interesting and somehow profound to my addled brain at the time.

When I finally got sober enough to say I was leaving, Dee instructed one of the men who had been there when I arrived to drive me home.

I figured it was because she wanted to know where I lived, so I had him drop me off several blocks from my apartment. I didn't think I ever wanted to see Dee or any of her friends again.

I stayed away—for a while.

But something about that place and that woman had gotten under my skin.

Distasteful as the experience had felt immediately after I left, the farther-removed in time I was from it, the more exotic and intriguing it seemed. Maybe just because I continued using meth, and my brain was losing all sense of what was real and what was imaginary.

A month or so later I looked up Dee's ad again, and this time my stay with her (actually her stay with me—I eventually ended up letting her move in with me) would last for two or more years. I don't know how long. One of the dark arts Dee practiced involved hanging people from the ceiling, encased in some sort of plastic bag, and feeding controlled amounts of intoxicants into the bag. People sometimes hung that way for days, totally unaware of the passage of time.

We were all trying, in some way, to escape this world and the pain it had caused us, and Dee was a walking encyclopedia of ways to help us do that.

I really don't know what all was going on, but I know there was identity theft involved. Dee and her associates probably drained the bank accounts of some of her clients.

I doubt that I had much in the bank for her to steal from me by the time I met her. Most of my money had been poured into The Beast, which now sat, unused and undrivable, in a shed in the back yard of a friend. I think Dee kept me around mainly for protection. Somehow she'd gotten ahold of the keys to my car, and I, the big, tough man, couldn't get up enough gumption to get them back from her.

So I stayed, most of the time in a drug-induced stupor, letting my life slip away, hoping it would soon be over. I honestly wanted to die, and I know that I overdosed several times, but something always brought me back to the land of the living.

It was during this time that I once again became aware of a quiet voice speaking to me from somewhere in the depths of my soul.

Words would come to me, and I would sit for hours, staring at the floor, running a single word through my mind over and over again like a mantra, pondering what it meant.

Some of these were words you'd only hear in church— the kind of place I'd seldom been to in the past forty years.

Somehow I sensed that these words, which had no meaning to me, still had significance, and I began to write them down on any scrap of paper that was at hand, spelling them out in whatever way seemed right to my muddled mind.

During the time that I was with Dee, I collected quite a pile of paper scraps, each with a word or two, or maybe a phrase scribbled on it in shaky, mostly illegible script. I kept them in plastic bags that I wouldn't let anyone else touch. They were some sort of treasure to me, something that had come to me from somewhere outside the debauched world I had descended into. They represented sanity to me, even though I didn't know what sanity was.

In their cumulative confusion, though, they began to speak to me.

As I sat, day after day, running them through my mind, herding them like cats, each with its own sense of purpose and destination, unable to be organized into any sensible form, they gradually brought me to the realization that I had to somehow escape the pit I was trapped in.

One day as I sat, stoned, in one of the dungeons where Dee serviced her clients, my frustration and desire to escape came to a head, and I went looking for my car keys, intent on getting away and somehow beginning to make sense of my life and my descent toward death. To do that I knew I needed to get away from the miasma that circulated around Dee, enveloping everyone who came near in a fog that kept them disoriented and unable to imagine a life outside her den of iniquity.

"Where are my keys?" I asked a man who sat in the lotus pose, staring into the smoky cloud filling the room. He didn't seem to know I was there. A naked woman sprawled on a futon. I shook her awake and asked for my keys. She just stared at me.

Dee came into the room then. "What are you seeking, little brother?" she asked in hypnotic tones. Long ago I had told her she was my big sister, my guide through life, and that I would be her little brother and protector.

On any other day, the question "What are you seeking" would have drawn me back under her spell, led me down a twisted path of unanswerable questions and koans, persuading me that I needed another hit of stimulant or hallucinogen to achieve enlightenment.

But not this day.

This day I somehow sensed that the answers lay not in chasing after her questions, but in the words that had been coming to me from another source. I had to pursue those answers, not her questions.

Dee lowered herself onto the floor in the middle of the room, her knees going akimbo toward the lotus position, and at that instant I let something happen that I had always resisted.

Having watched a series of men abuse my mother, I had resolved never to lay a violent hand on a woman. And I suppose that even now I technically stayed by my resolve.

I didn't touch her with my hands, but in an oft-practiced martial-arts move, I swung my right foot up to her throat and used it to push her down onto the floor, where she stared up at me, attempting to maintain the trance she had kept me in for so long. Her eyes at first refused to show fear, they remained placid, struggling for control, but as I pushed my heel into her windpipe, her face reddened, and she began to struggle to breathe.

With the slightest twitch I could have crushed her throat and ended her life.

But that was not my goal.

My goal was to end my own life.

But before I did that, I needed to find some answers.

I wouldn't find them as long as I remained under her control. I had to get out of there.

"You know who I am, and you know what I can do!"

I said it loud, and everyone in the room now began to emerge from their stupor, adrenaline somehow cutting through their drugged haze.

Fire came into Dee's eyes.

I relaxed some of the pressure on her throat, and she managed to croak out a threat. "You know who I am, Dragon!"

"Who are you?"

"I am the devil himself, and you will never escape my grasp!"

Her voice was unnaturally loud and deep. It didn't seem to be coming from her vocal chords.

"If you are the devil, then I am the Archangel!"

I didn't know it at the time, but my reference was to the apostle John's vision in Revelation, the last book of the Bible, of the Archangel Michael and his angels fighting Satan and his angels in heaven and casting them down to the earth. That imagery comes up in many occult teachings of the type Dee relished, so she understood the power I was claiming.

It silenced her. It was almost as though by calling myself the Archangel I had throttled the demons that drove her. She could not speak, could not summon the strength that had till now captivated me and kept me under her spell.

Had the demons been driven from the room by my invocation of the name of the Archangel, which in the Bible is synonymous with the name of Jesus Christ? I don't know. I wasn't intentionally invoking the name or power of God. As far as I knew, I was simply, in my ignorance of spiritual powers, asserting my own power over her.

It would be years later that I would finally come to understand the power of the name of Jesus; that I would be brought face to face with the One person who can deliver fallen, helpless, imprisoned humans from the demons that enslave them.

For the time, I saw only the physical battle that was being waged in that room.

I, Nico the Dragon, was asserting my manhood, reclaiming my life—or so I thought.

But something bigger was going on. A spiritual war.

Two powers were struggling for control of my soul.

On one side were the demons shouting at me, demanding that I destroy myself, driving me deeper and deeper into despair and debauchery. On the other, the still, small voice that had been whispering to me since I was a child.

"I am the Archangel!" I repeated, glaring into her eyes.

Nico the Dragon had everyone's attention now.

Nico the Dragon had always played the role of enforcer in that house. Nobody dared cross Dee the Dominatrix, or they would face the wrath of The Dragon.

Now the tables were turned, and the Dominatrix was under the heel of the Dragon.

Unbeknownst to me, an image from Genesis, the first book of the Bible, was being played out. When Adam and Eve were cast out of the Garden of Eden, the Lord promised them that the Serpent who had tempted them would bruise humanity's heel, but that the Scion of their race would bruise the Serpent's head—striking a fatal blow.

Now my heel rested on the neck of the Serpent Temptress. I thought it was happening in my own power. Looking back I know it was only in a power from outside myself that I was able to assert my independence and escape the bite of her fatal fangs.

My eyes locked on hers, and she blinked.

I looked up, then turned my glare on the half-dozen other people in the room, one by one, until each of them looked down, averting their eyes.

"I want to see my car keys in plain sight!" I roared.

No one moved.

"You know who I am, and what I can do!"

Everyone seemed to be entranced by something at their feet. No one would look up at me.

"Unless I see my keys in plain sight, I am going to take this place and everybody in it off its foundation!" Where did that threat come from? We were in an apartment building. Even big, tough Nico couldn't knock the place off its concrete slab. But the message got through.

I heard the jingle of keys. I looked down at Dee again, forcing my will on her, and finally she closed her eyes.

Only then did I relax the pressure on her neck and look up.

My keys lay on a low table.

Wordlessly I straightened to my full height, walked to the table, bent down, took the keys in my hand, and walked out the door without looking back.

Chapter 10

I thought I had broken free of the powers that had enslaved me for so long.

That was the problem. I thought *I* had done it.

I still had so much to learn about the spiritual war that was going on behind the scenes.

I found lodging with an old friend, determined to live in his spare bedroom, alone, waging war on my addiction. I was going to clean up my act and make a new start on life.

But I was trying to do it in my own strength. The strength of Nico the Dragon who had pummeled many a human adversary into submission. I didn't know who I was really fighting, and my resolve proved powerless. I never really stopped using at all, and it didn't take long for my friend to realize what was going on. Soon he told me if that's the way I was going to live, I couldn't do it at his house.

Through friends I learned about a dealer up in Ventura, fifty miles up the coast, who wanted protection. I went up there and he invited me to come and stay at his girlfriend's apartment. It was in a nice complex, clean sidewalks, neighbors with little kids' toys stored on their balconies.

He told me I could stay there as long as I wanted—no rent, free meth. All I had to do was be his enforcer—make sure the "friends" who stopped by didn't try to crash there—tell them this isn't a hotel, you've got to leave—once they'd gotten their fix.

It wasn't long before I made other friends, including the cook—the guy who was manufacturing the meth. Together we worked out a deal that if he'd toss a few spare crystals my way, he could keep some for himself too, and sell them on the street. I'd protect him, and he'd make sure I got as much of my poison-of-choice as I wanted.

That arrangement lasted for probably a year or so. Finally the apartment building was foreclosed on, and everybody had to move out.

I moved back to L. A. and fell in with another guy who wanted my protection. It will come as no surprise to you to learn that he, too, was a meth dealer.

Free rent. Free drugs. Free sex. It was everything I could ask for—except freedom.

Most of that time is a blur in my memory. I couldn't tell you what I did all day if I tried.

At night I would often go out, prowling the streets. Sometimes I'd end up in altercations because I still considered myself the defender of women and children, and I'd intervene whenever I thought someone was being abused.

From time to time I found myself crossways to the law, and ended up in handcuffs, but somehow I came through it all without winding up in jail. Several times an officer who was ready to haul me to the slammer looked at me and said, "I don't know why I'm doing this, but I'm going to let you go with a warning. Clean up your act, Mr. Hill. You won't get a second chance."

But I did keep getting second chances. Somehow Providence seemed to have its hand over me, even while I was cavorting on the devil's playground. These days I often speak to youths who have ended up incarcerated for the very sorts of things I used to get away with. If I had ever been arrested myself, it would have been next to impossible for me to pass the background check needed to clear me to enter juvenile detention facilities and reach out to troubled young people.

Next I lived in Hollywood for a bit, but I was no longer

the high-roller that used to cruise the bars and clubs paying for everyone else's drinks. Now I barely scraped by on money I could make from doing a little sales work. I rented a derelict room in a place where everyone else was on drugs, just like me.

The words that had been haunting me kept coming during this time. I had no idea why, or what they meant, but I somehow sensed that they had value. When a word or phrase would keep running through my head, I would finally find a scrap of paper to scribble it on. By then I had several bags full of words.

But none of it made sense.

Imagine dumping a bag full of words on the table and trying to pull some meaning from the mess. My life and the scraps were in the same state—a miasmic, meaningless mess that seemed to have no purpose.

I needed to get my life in order, if I ever hoped to be able to put the bags of words in the right order. I needed to make another stab at getting clean.

A friend from my days as a martial-arts teacher offered me a place to stay, and I took him up on it, determined that now, at last, I would be free. He was a police department watch commander, after all. There was no way I was going to do drugs while staying at his place, was there?

Yes, there was.

And when he realized what was going on, he was kind enough not to arrest me, but to simply help me move on. He knew jail wasn't the solution I needed. So he just told me I needed to find someplace else to stay while I got my life in order.

A friend helped me find the place in Koreatown where, eventually, after two more years of trying to destroy myself, I began to come to my senses and realize that I was never going to get my act together in my own strength.

Chapter 11

I sat on the back porch of my apartment in Koreatown, spewing words that I didn't understand, in sentences that didn't seem to have any right order or reason. But the words wouldn't leave me alone.

They were still in their plastic bags, scrawled on bits and scraps of paper, and I had been taking them out one by one and looking at them, trying to make sense of them.

Now they were beginning to form themselves into rhythmic phrases, something like musical rap. But none of it had any meaning to me.

The house was a big, ugly brick cube that had once had four nice, pleasantly-appointed apartments, complete with garden windows looking out on the world. Two apartments upstairs and two down.

The upstairs apartments could be accessed either by front steps that opened into their living rooms, or by a back set of wooden steps, leading directly into the kitchen.

A small porch at the top of the wooden steps was shared by the two upstairs apartments.

The building was in total disrepair. The downstairs by now was totally wrecked, its shattered windows boarded up. Transients often broke in and camped out there for days at a time without interference. The smell of urine, rotting food, marijuana fumes, and excrement often seeped into the apartments upstairs, but I didn't really care. I was living there simply waiting to die.

The words were flowing, and I was staring with bleary eyes into L. A.'s gray-blue sky, when the one sane person in my life came trotting up the wooden steps, on his way home from his day job as a waiter at a nearby restaurant.

Steve is a writer. He's had his hand on several movie scripts, but like the majority of people involved in the movie industry, he needed another job to keep money coming in on a regular basis.

When he got to the top of the stairs, he stopped and just stood there watching me and listening. I didn't pay any attention to him. My mind was totally absorbed in the words that kept flowing.

"You've really got something there," Steve said.

I slowly lowered my head and tried to get my eyes to focus on his face.

"What?"

"I said you've really got something there."

"You think?"

"Say that again, what you just said."

When I did, he said, "Hold that thought," and unlocked his back door, went into the kitchen, and brought out a chair and sat down across from me.

We hadn't talked much in the past. We'd say neighborly greetings from time to time, and occasionally when I would be in one of my rants, making too much noise on the back porch, probably cursing somebody out on the telephone, he'd come out and try to calm me down. "You can't be shouting four-letter-words all over the neighborhood," he'd say. "Somebody's gonna call the cops."

For some reason I respected Steve, and didn't give him any guff when he spoke to me that way. My whole persona in that hood was based on fierceness. I considered myself the protector of the area—I'd stare down and chase away evil in any form that offended me (which of course didn't include drug trafficking).

People didn't cross me—any that did, didn't do it twice.

But for some reason Steve, who's not a very big or tough guy, had the guts to stand up to me and tell me when I was out of line. And I respected him for it. Now he was sitting down with me on our shared back porch and telling me that I had something worthwhile in the words that were spilling out of the garbage bags in my house, and out of the wreck of a human being that I had become.

"What do you mean?" I asked.

"That's good stuff you're reciting."

"It is?"

"Yeah. I can see deep meaning in it."

"Really?"

"Yeah. Keep working on it."

"You're the writer."

"Yeah."

"And you think what I'm saying is good stuff."

"I don't just think it's good stuff, I know it's good stuff. You must be a modern-day prophet or something."

I just stared at him, my vision still blurry. He was completely the opposite of me, but for some reason I respected him.

He sat, letting me stare at him for a minute or two, then got up, picked up his chair, reached out and put a hand on my shoulder. "It might be your redemption," he said, then went inside.

I slumped back in my chair.

What had just happened?

It didn't make any more sense to me than the words I kept repeating. But Steve saw meaning in it all.

That was the beginning of a very special relationship— not that we ever became close, fast friends—but Steve became my sounding board.

Like most writers with any reputation in Hollywood, Steve is constantly hounded by people with "great ideas" they want him to listen to, and maybe write up for them. He doesn't have much patience with such things. "If it's such a great idea, sit down and write it up yourself," is his standard response before drawing a line through their name on his list of friends he wants to spend time with.

Neither of us can really explain why he had so much

patience with me. He tells me today he can't count the number of hours he spent listening to me.

It would always start with a knock on his back door. "Hey Steve, you gotta hear this," I'd say.

"I'm busy, Nico. I've got to get my own writing done."

"Just two minutes. Listen for just two minutes. That's all it'll take. I promise."

"All right, Nico, let me hear what you've got."

I'd start reciting one of my poems that I had begun to call "The Spoken Word," and I'd make a mistake a minute or two in, and stop and say "That's not right. Let me start again."

"No! Just pick up from where you left off," Steve would plead.

"No, no, I've got to start from the beginning."

For some reason I couldn't pick up in the middle, I always had to say the whole piece that I was working on. Half-an-hour later, I'd probably finally make it all the way through.

But Steve was always patient. "I just saw something in you Nico," he told me years later. "Something that was coming out of you had the power to touch people, and I hoped it was going to touch you too, maybe help you dig yourself out of the pit you'd dug for yourself."

The place we were living really was the pits at that time.

I wouldn't leave because I was comfortable there, and because I didn't want to move my cat Squeaky to a new place. She is a feral cat that I had adopted several years earlier, and every time I moved to a new place she had trouble adjusting. I didn't want to have to worry about her getting out and getting lost in an unfamiliar neighborhood. She was the one stable thing that had stuck with me through all my moving about and self-destructive behavior. I couldn't bear to lose her.

Steve wouldn't leave because he had another plan in mind. He knew that the landlord wasn't making payments on the mortgage, and that sooner or later the building would be sold to someone who would redevelop it. And he knew that the new owners couldn't evict him. They'd have to continue to rent the renovated apartment to him for only slightly more than he was paying for the dump he was living in now—something about rent control laws.

For different reasons we both hung in there, in anything-but-ideal conditions. And over the course of those two years as neighbors, we formed a weird sort of partnership.

I thought of myself as the guardian angel for that property—chasing away any ne'er-do-wells that tried to encroach on our space.

Today I realize that Steve was, in a different way, a guardian angel for me.

Chapter 12

When I first moved into the apartment in Koreatown, I had no idea I would find a guardian angel there, but that is what Steve became to me.

The other people living there certainly didn't qualify as angels.

A hulking older man whose arms were covered in prison tats already occupied part of the apartment I was living in. I'll call him Lucky, but he wasn't my guardian angel, that honor I give to Steve, the guy in the other apartment who would listen to my Spoken Word.

The apartment I moved into had six rooms altogether. Lucky occupied two of them, and I took two others. Other people would sometimes move into the remaining space. One fellow was there for quite a while, a reformed gang banger I'll call Eddie.

Though we shared the apartment, the three of us all kept pretty much to ourselves.

Word on the street was that Lucky was a former leader of one of L. A.'s toughest gangs who'd spent much of his life in prison, and was only out on the streets now because of a governor's pardon—due to his failing physical condition. He was still a big, strong guy, but he walked with a cane due to having had his hip broken at some time.

I had very little respect for him, because I thought he was a hypocrite. He made money on the side by selling marijuana. But if you wanted to buy from him, you first had to sit and listen to him read to you from the Bible. I didn't know a lot about the Bible at the time, but somehow that just didn't seem right to me.

I'm not sure how Eddie survived. Maybe doing odd jobs, and no doubt selling some drugs on the side when he could get enough cash together to get a supply.

The three of us shared the apartment, the bathroom, and the kitchen, but never spent any time hanging out together. We each had a series of locks on the doors to our private quarters, and it was known that we would not under any circumstances enter each other's rooms without an invitation.

The day I moved in, Lucky knocked on my door and looked me over. He must have thought I was okay, because he just nodded and grunted. "Watch out for Jesse," he said. "Don't let him shaft you."

"No worries, man," I said. He just moseyed back down the hall and shut his door behind him.

A few days later I found out what he'd meant.

Jesse was the guy who rented the room to me. The house actually belonged to his mother, and he was living in part of the wrecked space on the ground floor, in a room with boarded up windows and furniture he'd found abandoned on the street.

I paid him two months' rent in cash when I moved in. Three days later he was at my door, explaining that there were some unexpected expenses, and I needed to give him $200 to cover them.

When I told him I didn't have any money to give him, he looked me over sharp-eyed and tried to look past me into my room to see if there was anything he could hock for me, but I was a good six inches taller than him, and I made sure he couldn't see past me.

The next day he was at the door again. "You can't pay, you have to get out. So go. I want you out by tonight."

I just laughed at him and closed the door in his face.

Several days later he was back, this time with an off-duty policeman friend of his in tow. "This guy isn't paying his rent," he claimed, then looked at me. "You got to get out, Nico."

"I paid him two months' rent in advance," I told the officer. "Cash."

"He says you didn't."

"I says I did." I drew myself up to my full height.

The officer looked me over. He knew he had no right to try to enforce his friend's wishes, and he wasn't about to try strong-arming me. "His word against yours," he said to Jesse, and turned to go.

Jesse had the narrow eyes and pointed nose of a rat. Now his eyes went to tiny slits as he jutted out his chin and looked me up and down before following his friend down the steps. "I'll be back. You'll see."

When I saw Lucky on the street later that day, he said "I see Jesse came by. You stayin'?"

"You bet I am. I paid my rent."

"You ain't the first one he's tried this on. Only reason he hasn't thrown me out is 'cause he feels sorry for me, maybe. I dunno, probably doesn't feel anything really. You're the first one stand up to him. He's rented those rooms more times than the Red Sox lost the pennant. Pockets the cash, then scares 'em away."

"I don't scare easy."

"He's got friends, you know."

"I don't scare easy," I repeated.

I didn't just stand up to Jesse, I eventually took matters into my own hands. None of the other people living there wanted him around, because he kept hassling them for more money that they didn't owe him. His mother had let him stay there with the understanding that he'd collect the rent, but I doubt she ever saw the money he collected, and he kept hitting people up for even more.

Finally I got really tired of that, and I broke into his room and started moving everything out into the dilapidated garage beside the building. When he came back, he could see what had happened, and he figured he knew who was behind it. When he came knocking, I just told him,

"Nobody wants you around here, so get lost. I can be rain, or I can be thunder and lightning. I ever see you around here again, you know what it'll be."

"You think you're so tough!" he said, and just then my cat Squeaky brushed up against my leg. He feinted toward her, like he was going to strangle her. Instantly my fist hit the wall beside the door, shattering plaster and the wood lath behind it.

Jesse jumped backwards several inches and watched with bulging eyes as I pulled my bloodied fist out of the wall, then he turned and slunk down the stairs. I think I saw a wet spot expanding down the inside of one of his pants legs as he went.

About that time I quit paying rent, so he sent a burly friend of his by to try to scare me. That didn't work. As I said, I don't scare easy. The big guy left, and I knew I wouldn't be seeing him coming around again.

In my own eyes I began to see myself as the defender of the downtrodden living there. I set myself up as some sort of Robin Hood hero, but really I was just a crook shafting another crook.

When Jesse kept trying to have me evicted, I came up with a dishonest scheme to get him off my back for good. It involved having a crooked friend draw up a lease agreement, indicating that two years of rent had been paid in advance, then forging Jesse's signature and getting another friend to notarize his signature and mine. I did the same for Lucky and Eddie.

Next time Jesse came by with the police to try to evict us, I showed the officer the signed lease. "I didn't sign that!" Jesse exclaimed, his rat eyes bulging.

"Your word against his," the officer said, and that put an end to Jesse's harassment.

But there was another type of harassment that couldn't be ended so easily.

Four years earlier I had set out on a path of self-destruction. I made a conscious choice to walk away from life as I had known it, with the goal of descending as far into the abyss of sin and self-abuse as possible, on my way to an early grave.

The drugs I was taking were part of that plan.

The times I tried to break free came in brief flashes of sanity that never lasted more than a few days.

By the time I arrived at the apartment in Koreatown, I had given up on ever finding peace and a normal life again.

The only ray of light breaking through into the dark dungeon I had created for myself was the words.

The words I kept in garbage bags, and only occasionally poured out to try to bring some order into my world.

As I remember those days and nights, it was all one long trip, always on drugs. But that's not the way it was in reality. There were times when I was in my right mind and seemed like a fairly normal guy. The only way I know that is because people like Steve, and my former boss Greg, have told me so. Steve says he knew I must be doing drugs at times, but usually when he would see me, I seemed fairly normal. I seemed to be able to hide the symptoms of addiction on days when I wasn't high. We'd exchange neighborly greetings if he saw me during the day. If he saw me going out at night, though—all dressed in black, looking like I was looking for trouble—he'd just nod and hurry past.

At the time I was getting a small public assistance check, and had a card that would let me buy $200 worth of groceries every month. The cash I got all went for drugs. Sometime during that period I got hit by a car while crossing the street. I wasn't hurt bad, but it was enough to get me a $5,000 settlement. Steve was a good enough friend to drive me to several appointments to work out the details of getting that cash—which was enough to fuel my drug use for quite a while.

Another time Steve found me mowing the grass around our building. I think it was at the time when we knew the place was being foreclosed on, and a buyer was going to be coming to look at it. Steve had told me that if a development company bought the place, they would want to renovate it, and we'd get a cash settlement if we had to move out.

That sounded good to me, so I guess I got it in my mind that the place needed to look a little better to help the sale go down.

The building and grounds hadn't been maintained for years. The grass was two feet tall, bushes had grown up so high that you couldn't even see the second story windows, and street people would sometimes camp out between the bushes and the building.

There was no lawnmower, but I had a knife with a six-inch blade. Steve remembers coming home one summer afternoon when it was over a hundred degrees, and there was The Dragon, down on his hands and knees with this knife, mowing the grass, inch by inch. He asked if I'd had anything to eat or drink that day, and I told him no, so he went down the street and got me two burgers, a soda, and a big milkshake. That's how great a guy my guardian angel is.

I saw Greg, my former boss, several times as well—he was no longer living in the area, but would stop by when he was in town—and I'd usually cadge a "loan" from him, which he knew wasn't a loan at all. The money was going for drugs, but until he told a mutual friend about how much weight I had lost, Greg had no clue about my addiction. I was looking like a skeleton by then, at about 155 pounds, down from 210. The friend, without even seeing me, diagnosed my addiction and told Greg about it. Still Greg had a hard time believing I was a down-and-out addict. So I guess I put on a pretty good front whenever I went out in public.

Recently I stopped by to visit with another friend in Koreatown, a really nice guy who runs a local convenience store. We reminisced about one time when he'd seen me out on the street, having a hard time walking, and he'd helped me make it the three blocks to my apartment. "What was going on with you that day, Nico?" he asked me when we were together again.

"I was coming down off a high," I told him.

"I didn't even know you were a user," he confessed.

On the outside I could fool people.

On the inside I was playing the fool.

On the outside people still saw the tough guy who could scare away evil.

On the inside I was the slave to evil.

People who saw me walking down the street would avert their eyes if there was anything nefarious in their plans for the day. They knew The Dragon as the guy who wouldn't tolerate abuse or misuse of the people in his 'hood.

If they could have seen The Dragon in his lair, enslaved by addiction, tormented by demons, chained to a death wish, they would have known the real Nico.

But I had learned early in my life, at the end of my father's switch, not to let anyone really know me, not to let them see inside.

Chapter 13

Inside my two rooms was where the real me lived. The enslaved, chained Dragon, waiting for his own extinction. And not just waiting. Actively pursuing it. Hating himself. Hating what he had become, yet at the same time feeling a sense of triumph.

I was well on my way to accomplishing what I had set out to do—destroy myself.

It seems hard to believe that a man could hate himself so much that he would want to take all the rage he felt against the world that had treated him badly and torture himself with it.

My mother committed suicide at age 58, while working at a suicide-prevention center. I was never told exactly how she did it—it happened while I was still making movies and doing cage fights. One of my championship belts had a plaque with her name on it, because I dedicated that fight in 1999 to her memory.

She was a tortured soul, I suppose. I hadn't had a lot of contact with her during those days when I was living the high life. But she didn't feel the need to torture herself to death. Whatever she did to end her own life, it was probably quick and painless.

I had talked to her a few days before she took that final step, and I noticed she didn't sound like her normal self. My brother usually went to see her fairly often, but the last time he went, she wouldn't even let him into the apartment.

He had a little bit of a cold, and she said she didn't want to catch it from him.

A few days later I called her. I was working on a movie being shot in Malibu at the time, and she was living in Los Angeles, so I offered to come by for a visit, but she seemed very hesitant to have me come. She was answering hotline calls for a suicide-prevention agency at the time, and totally immersed in her work.

I told her I was coming, but when she was so hesitant, I decided not to waste my time driving into town, only to have her refuse to come to the door, so I didn't go. It was a couple weeks later that I was contacted with the news that her body had been found in her apartment, probably several days after she had taken her life.

It seemed so ironic. She had tried to help others cling to life, but had given up on it herself. She never was terribly religious, but had been into all kinds of New Age things. She did palm reading, numerology, and astrology, but every week she would watch the Christian program *Hour of Power* on TV and call the prayer hotline to ask for prayer.

I guess she was conflicted inside, and life eventually got to be too much to handle. At some point she snapped and took her life quickly.

I was never able to take that route. For some reason I felt the need to kill myself slowly and painfully.

You can psychoanalyze me any way you want—say that my behavior was a reaction to my childhood when my anger at how I was being treated fused together with my desire to protect my mother and my hatred of myself for not being able to do it. But really, there's no rational explanation for what I was doing. I know now that there were spiritual powers fighting for control, spiritual beings who are fighting a much larger war for control of everyone on this planet. But at the time I couldn't explain what was going on inside my head, or what I was doing to myself.

When it came to drugs, I would use whatever was available, no questions asked. Crack cocaine—cut or uncut. It's supposed to be diluted with baking soda; if you use it straight, I was told, it can easily kill you. Do you think I cared? Of course not. That's what I wanted.

It burned through the membranes in my throat, my nose, even my eyes. I believe the white powder I saw on my face the day I saw a ghost in the mirror had been deposited there as fumes seeped through my burned-out membranes onto my skin.

At times my face felt like it was being stung by a thousand bees; electrical shocks made my cheeks, chin, and eyes twitch, but pain couldn't put the brakes on my slide into the abyss. It was all part of my plan.

I had been instructed to never inhale cocaine fumes into my lungs—it could freeze them. Did that stop me?

Dee once told me that her suppliers were putting embalming fluid into the meth she was supplying me with— it would eventually close off my wind pipes and keep me from being able to breathe. So what? Isn't that what I wanted—to stop breathing?

The physical abuse I was heaping on myself didn't end with smoking, snorting, and drinking meth. I hated myself enough that I would look in the mirror, then punch myself in the face. Many times I woke up on the floor with a broken nose or black eye, wondering what had happened, then realizing I had knocked myself out. In the battle of life I was fighting on both sides and winning and losing at the same time.

This went on for years.

There is no good physical explanation for why I never ended up dead or a derelict living on the streets, but one way or another I stayed alive and managed to keep a roof over my head. Looking back now, I can't help but believe that there was a purpose in it all—not that the spiritual powers on the side of good in the world would have led me into the depths that I descended to—I did that myself, under the influence of very different spirits. But the fact that I went into those depths and didn't lose my life—that makes me think that my neighbor Steve wasn't the only guardian angel operating in my life.

Amidst the cacophony of voices in my head, calling me to destroy myself, the small voice I had heard as a child continued to speak, whispering among the shouts, and somehow in my saner moments I continued to listen.

The words, scrawled in barely-legible script on scraps of paper, filled garbage bags in my room, and when I would take them out and look at them, they gradually began to form themselves into semi-meaningful phrases and sentences that took on a rhythm something like what you hear from rappers like Eminem or Tupac, but without so much harshness or negative focus.

I would sit on my back porch, running these phrases over and over through my mind, speaking them aloud as they took shape. Then I'd knock on Steve's door and say "You gotta hear this man," and he would patiently listen and keep encouraging me to listen to my own words, to pursue a better, more rational and meaningful life through them.

The words gradually began to take on meaning to me, and I gave the phenomenon that I didn't fully understand a name: "The Spoken Word." They seemed to take on special power when spoken, so I would recite them over and over again.

The words would come out late at night, too, while I was wandering the dim streets, telling myself that I was out there as the protector or guardian angel to the prostitutes and runaways that shared the shadows with me.

Sometimes when I would spot a derelict addict sprawled in a doorway, I would stop and look at him or her and share.

Here I am and I choose to stand alone.
The innocent cries from my mother's womb.
To the man that's standing here right before you
That slowly gave away pieces of his very own soul.
The colors drift in and out of my mind,
The music plays but is so out of time.

Please don't ask me why.
But when I lay down tonight,
I will never again awake to cry.
So take me away to a place I know I can be,
Take me away to a place you prepared with your own hands,
That I will never want to leave.

And you said to go and find the wise one.
And when you do, ask him if there was really a plan, purpose,
or mission
For someone like me to do,
How long before I was to realize,
that that wise man was in your word, your truth, your light, your
sacrifice, and your salvation.
And it's always and forever been you.
And yet here I am and I am still all alone.

The words might not seem to make a lot of sense as you see them on paper, but they came out of my mouth with a rhythm and conviction that somehow always penetrated the haze filling the minds of lost souls like myself. "How do you know me so well—have you been following me?" they might say. Some would break out in tears, "I can't believe you understand me. That's me. How do you know me so well?"

When the tears came, I would share another of my Spoken Words:

They came early in the morning.
There was no kind of warning.
They viciously meticulously,
Ripped away my everything then drawn under lock and key.
Someone like you and me.
They stripped me of my very right to be free
And though I committed no crime at all,
they soon found me guilty of breaking a manmade law.

But I am you and you are me.
They can never have the precious times or share our strong
faith.
Or our vivid memories.
So please do not be afraid to cry.
If that helps the sadness I last saw in your eye.
But as for me this is not goodbye until we meet again as one.
Celebrating our freedom and the end of man's tyranny and
oppression. …

And if my spirit could be broken
With the words that were spoken
They came to me in hopes that this would make me lose my
mind.
They said to me, No more sunshine
Only rain, death, and prison time
No more sunshine until the very day,
In the name of oppression and by their tyranny
They come and carry my worthless body away

So now please tell my people for me
When I am put in my cage,
Instead of rage
I now pray.
Tell them to let it rain, let it rain all night and day.
For this is what will wash our sins away.
Tell them to let it rain, let it rain till the very end.
For this will fill the river of redemption.
To which we will wade in.

Tell them to go find the field of pain.
To walk past the man that dons the black mask.
And refuse any shovel of disdain.
Get down on their knees and dig until their knuckles are
bloody.
That is where they will find my spirit.
As promised we will meet as one under the sun.

CALLED FROM THE ABYSS

Celebrating our freedom,
And the end of tyranny and oppression.

Some thanked me. Others reacted with anger, shouting at me, telling me they wished I was dead.

I feared none of them. The spirit within me compelled me to go out at night, seeking the most evil and nefarious denizens of the darkness and speak to them.

Whatever their reaction, I would leave them to ponder what they had heard on their own. It wasn't like I was a missionary trying to rescue them from their tormented lives. It was only that I felt compelled to share what the voice within had spoken to me. Whether it made any difference in their lives did not concern me.

Remembering those difficult days, I hope that perhaps I may have pointed at least a few of those souls in a direction that would lead them out of the darkness.

As for me, despite the words I spoke to others, I continued my downward spiral, and finally I arrived at the day I had pursued for so long.

I saw the ghost in the mirror, the ghost of the man I had once been. As I looked at him, the voices that had been shouting at me for so long, egging me on in my fight against myself, cried out louder and louder *Do it! Do it! Strike that last blow and the fight will be over!*

Back in my rooms, I closed up my cat Squeaky in a place where she would not witness the end, then thrashed about the room, smashing the remnants of everything I had not destroyed before.

Except for the two glass pipes that were to be the conduit of death I would smoke as my final act on earth.

My mission was to destroy everything I owned, then to get to the drugs.

I fell to my knees on the broken glass, then picked up one of the pipes I had been careful to save. My hands were shaking. They always shook in those days, I was used to it.

I found the little bag that had my last stash of meth and

carefully, ever-so-carefully poured it into the bowl at the end of the pipe.

"Do it, Nico! Do it! Faster! Do more! This is your time!" The demons surrounding me continued to torment me and cheer me on.

"What do you want?" I shouted back at them. "I'm doing as much as I can as fast as I can! What do you want me to do? Get a knife and slit my throat? I won't do that!"

I don't know why I wouldn't do that—I don't know what was going through my head. But for some reason, even in my most distraught state, even in my deepest despair, I wouldn't do that.

A cigarette lighter shook in my hands as I fumbled with the flint, trying to get it to light so I could turn the meth into the vapor that would release me from my pain.

And that's when I heard the quiet voice.

"Is this what you want, then, Nico? For them to find you, just another burned out addict, lying on the floor, eyes staring into heaven in search of salvation you will never find, garbage on your right, garbage on your left, garbage for your bed? The demons you have fought will have won, and they will go on to more conquests. They will inhabit the lives of those who find you. Is that what you want? Really?

"Is that what you want? Really?

"Is that what you want? Really?"

The question echoed over and over in my mind.

My glassy eyes struggled to focus.

I saw the pipe; I saw the lighter; I saw my hands shaking as they struggled to perform their last act.

Their last act. Did I really want that to be the last act they performed?

I didn't know.

I didn't think so...

I was a fighter. Did my fight really have to be against myself?

The tension that had raged through my body slowly began to relax.

My hands still shook, but, other than the shaking, they

were still. I was no longer trying to get a flame started under the glass bowl.

My fingers relaxed. The lighter dropped, then the pipe, breaking into a dozen pieces, spraying its lethal dose of crystals over the detritus of a shattered life, and I crumpled to the floor, weeping, and lapsed mercifully into unconsciousness.

Some people will crawl inside to hide.
While others are two-faced, content to live that lie.
Still others make the big mistake.
You cannot return from what we call that suicide.
But as for you and I,
I would rather fight than die.

What is your affliction, for we all have an addiction?
Whether you walk right in with a wink, smile, or holding a prescription.
What is it that you do, do you do it, or does it master you?
There is a sensation that starts at our creation.
It is called self-mutilation.
If you want to know who is asking, just look in the mirror.
That is my true assassin, it always follows me,
It forecasts my true enemy.

I had often recited those spoken words to others.

As I gradually became aware of myself lying broken and bleeding on shards of glass and garbage, they were playing through my mind.

"I would rather fight than die."

Would I really?

"If you want to know who is asking, just look in the mirror.

"That is my true assassin, it always follows me,

"It forecasts my true enemy."

The words had often flowed from my mouth without understanding. I had thought they were for others. I had sought out those I thought were the lowest forms of life on the human totem pole and preached those words to them.

But they were meant for me.

Suddenly I realized they were all meant for me.

They described me, not some drug pusher or derelict drunk.

They were addressed to Nico, and I needed to understand them. I needed to understand why I, like the people I had preached to, had become my own worst enemy.

"I wrote God's Soldier on your heart," the quiet voice said. "Is this how you want to die? Fighting against yourself?"

"No, I don't."

"I called you to fight against evil, to help others escape its grasp. You can't do that if you're dead."

"No, I can't."

"Then what are you going to do about it?"

"Can I really—can I rescue others?"

"Not if you destroy yourself."

That was the most rational thought I had had in a very long time.

"Is that you God? Is it you that's been talking to me in that quiet voice all this time?"

No voice answered. It was up to me to find the answer. "Okay God. I hear your voice. I know what you want me to do. I guess I've known it for a long time. But I don't have peace of mind."

I sat up and looked at the wreckage around me and realized that it represented my soul. Chaos and turmoil had ruled me for longer than I could remember.

"I don't have peace of mind, and I don't have anywhere to go."

I lay back down on my bed of glass and garbage, feeling sorry for myself and who I had become, but the voices were silent. All of them.

If I picture in my mind what was going on in that war-torn, storm-ravaged room, I see demons on one side, their mouths hanging open, their eyes darting fire and hate, yelling and screaming at me to go on and just get it over with.

And on the other side of the room I see a Man on a Hill, his arms outstretched, blood dripping from his hands. His eyes are soft with tears as he looks across the room, but in his look is power. The power to give others hope. The power of love.

Who would blink?

Who would look down?

The battle was set. The cage was closed. And the one who blinked first would lose.

Chapter 14

In the Bible there is the story of a storm that nearly swallowed the twelve men who had been called to spread a message of hope and God's love to the world, ending their mission before it had even started.

A deadly, destructive storm had raged in my life for fifty years, and on that day it had nearly swallowed me. As I tell you the Bible story, as I envision it, I think you will see why it resonates with me, explains myself to me, *and* gives me hope.

The story has two main characters and a cast of thousands.

The protagonist is, as you might expect, Jesus Christ.

The antagonist doesn't get a name. His moniker is "a man out of the tombs."

Get it? He was a walking dead man—not a zombie or something mythical like that, just a man who was still alive, but living like he was dead. Probably wishing he was dead. Pale, skeletal, shaking, mumbling, stumbling. A mirror image of Nico the Dragon at his lowest moment.

Tombs in that part of the world are caves cut into solid rock, so we're not talking about some half-alive wraith lurking around headstones and hiding behind monuments to the departed. We're talking about a man who has chosen to depart from civilized society and to exist only in darkness, out of sight and out of mind, perhaps even gnawing on the bones of the dead.

As you know, in any good story the protagonist and antagonist must finally come face to face in a showdown where only one of them can triumph.

Tomb Man had been running from that encounter all his life.

But one day, at the end of a long day of preaching to thousands of people who had thronged to see him on the west side of a lake known as the Sea of Galilee, Jesus looked across to the eastern shore and said to his disciples "Let's take a little ride, over to the other side." Galilee is really just a wide spot in the south-flowing River Jordan, a few miles across.

Several of his disciples were professional fishermen, so the idea of a night on the lake was nothing new to them. That was their usual time to be afloat.

Cramming thirteen men into one of the little fishing boats that was usually manned by only two might have seemed risky, but when Jesus made a suggestion, there was always a good reason behind it, so apparently nobody questioned him.

Until the storm came up, that is.

The Sea of Galilee is surrounded by steep hills on every side, and as night falls and the air cools, the wind coming down off the hills can suddenly become fierce, almost cyclonic. And that's what happened that night.

Theirs wasn't the only boat on the lake, but theirs was probably the most overloaded. With calm water just inches from the gunwales, they were in danger as soon as things started to stir.

Soon there was water in the bottom of the boat, and they were bailing hard. It was a hopeless task, though. They were sinking and sinking fast. So, what was Jesus doing— he who had set them out on this mission in the first place?

He'd worked hard all day, and he was tired. The gentle swell of the calm sea had lulled him to sleep, and there he was, still resting in the back of the boat, not lifting a finger to help; sleeping through his corps' demise.

When they shook him awake, shouting in his ear "Don't

you care that we're about to die?" he looked around and shrugged, wondering why these followers of his were bothered by something so small as a storm on a tiny lake.

"Peace, be still," Jesus said, and in a few moments the winds died down, and the sea that had been tossing them, threatening to drown them, resumed its gentle rocking. And there they were, alone on the silent sea. The other boats, not overloaded like theirs, had no doubt beat for shore quickly, as soon as trouble started brewing.

As I lay on my bed of glass and garbage that day in Koreatown, a quiet peace, an eerie silence, descended on the room.

There was no one else there with me.

Lucky and Eddie, who had been in their own rooms earlier, had bailed. They wanted no part of the storm raging around Nico.

Alone on the peaceful, windless sea, the disciple corps and their master moseyed slowly to the far side, to the appointment Jesus had set out to fulfill.

Day had broken by time they made landfall.

Jesus had directed them to a secluded spot.

He had felt eyes watching him as they drifted toward that rendezvous.

The man behind the eyes had sensed that the dawning day would be momentous for him. Something about the boat that had set its course for his domain spoke to him.

Voices in his head spoke words that seemed to have no meaning, but they would not be silent. This was nothing new to him. For years he had lived this way, tormented by words and images that seized control of his soul and would not let him live as a real human being.

They drove him to the shadows, lurked with him in the corners and in the tombs, terrifying all who saw him.

More than that, they empowered him.

Fear breeds power, and though the villagers in the area may have wished him dead, they dared not be the ones to cast the stones. Rather, they tried to bind him, shackle him, chain him down. But pain was nothing to him. He loathed himself so deeply that cutting his flesh with sharp stones was child's sport to him. Given enough time, he would wiggle and wrestle himself free, bloodied but breathing, from all restraints.

And so they let him live among the tombs, hoping for the day when he would take up permanent residence with the rest of the dead.

The bow of the boat ground into the water-smoothed stones of the narrow beach, and the man-out-of-the-tombs emerged into shadows cast by the west-facing cliffs into which his home was cut, inching forward and downward for a better view.

Jesus was the last one off the boat, and as he stood on the rocky shore, he looked up into the hills, toward the tombs, and saw the man with whom he had an appointment. He'd come all this way, weathered the storm, calmed the sea, all for this one man.

All the elements of earth had conspired together to try to prevent this meeting, but they had bowed to the power of the man who had come to bring peace on earth.

The two warriors advanced upon each other, Jesus climbing slowly up the hill, Tomb Man, inching his way out of the shadows, until suddenly the spirits controlling him sent him in a mad dash down the hill, shouting at the top of his lungs, "What do you want with me, Jesus Son of the Most High God? I beg you. For the sake of God, don't torment me! I've suffered enough already!" It wasn't his voice speaking. It wasn't his words coming out of his mouth. It was the powers that had commandeered his soul years ago, as he had descended into debauchery and self-destructive deeds. I know how that can happen to a man, because it happened to me.

Jesus had been saying quietly, as he climbed to the rendezvous, "Come out of the man, you unclean spirit," and the spirit (demons, actually) had been compelled to listen. They had no recourse but to—like the winds on the sea—

obey. But they would not go willingly. They had tormented and terrified the people of this region for years, and they liked the neighborhood. They would do everything in their power to avoid eviction. Terror was their stock in trade, and so they seized the man, enraged him, and sent him flying headlong down the hill to frighten Jesus away.

But Jesus didn't scare easily.

The fiery passion roiling in Tomb Man's eyes could not make him blink.

"What's your name?" Jesus asked as calmly as he had said "Peace be still," a few hours earlier.

The voices answered truthfully, something they weren't accustomed to doing, but were now compelled to do. "My name is Legion, for we are many!"

In those days if you heard that a Roman Legion was headed your way, it was time to skedaddle. Head for the hills and hunker down till they were gone. Those who resisted their advance usually ended up dead.

Scare Jesus away, that was their strategy.

But Jesus didn't scare easily.

The disciples had all headed for the boat when they saw the man coming, and now they were calling to Jesus to "Get in! Let's get out of here!" They wanted to put as much water between themselves and Tomb Man as they could as quickly as they could.

But Jesus stood his ground.

The two men locked eyes: The one who had come from the darkness of the tomb, and the one had come from the radiance of heaven. And the man out of the tombs was the one who blinked.

He lowered his eyes and spoke in a barely-audible mumble. "All right. We get the picture. Just don't send us away. This is home to us. We like it here."

"Where would you like to go?" Jesus asked.

"There's pigs over there. We could live in them, couldn't we? Please?"

"If you wish," Jesus shrugged.

And with a shriek like a storm rending ragged cliffs, they

flew out of the man, leaving him trembling, lying on the ground wondering what had happened to him, and moved to their new residence. A herd of pigs that was being tended on the hillside.

In some ways animals are smarter than humans.

They know that life possessed by demons isn't worth living.

When the demons entered the pigs, they took off running down the hill, unwilling to live that way, and drowned themselves in the lake.

Which, of course, didn't sit well with the people who'd hired the herders to graze them there.

When news reached town, of what had just happened, do you suppose the people came out to thank Jesus for delivering the man of his demons?

No, they came out to assess the damage to their bank accounts, which had largely been invested in pigs.

Money talks, they say, and when they talked to Jesus, it was to ask him to kindly leave their territory before he did any more damage to the economy.

They didn't even seem to notice that Jesus was standing there, dressed only in his under garments—a long, gown-like single layer of linen—carrying on a rational conversation with the formerly-naked-and-irrational Tomb Man, who was wearing a nice robe—the one Jesus had taken off to give to him.

Jesus listened politely and turned to go to the boat. His mission wasn't to these people, not just now anyhow. He'd fulfilled the day's mission to that region when he'd rendezvoused with Tomb Man and set him free.

Tomb Man followed him down to the water's edge and begged to be allowed to get into the boat and go with Jesus and his disciples, but Jesus said no. He had other plans for this man he had risked life, limb, and mission to save from himself.

"Your mission is to go back where you came from, and tell the people there what I've done for you. Go back to the very people you once terrified; the very people who are in the thralls of demon possession, even if they aren't so destroyed as you, and tell them that they too can be free in the name of Jesus. Find the downcast, the downtrodden, the debauched and despairing, and tell them to look up. There is a man coming for them, a man on a mission to deliver them.

"And after you've done that, I'll be back.

"Tell them I'm coming back.

"That's your mission. That will keep you from falling back into your old ways. By saving others, you will save yourself."

Chapter 15

Nico the Dragon had been called out of his lair by the same voice that called Tomb Man out from his dark haunts.

Somehow I knew that, even though I wasn't familiar with the story from the Bible, and knew about as much about God and Jesus as I did about unicorns.

"Okay God, I hear your voice," I said quietly into the peace that had descended. "I know what you want me to do. I've known for a long time what you wanted me to do. But I don't know peace of mind, and I don't want to be here. I don't even want to be alive." I paused and thought long and hard about what I was saying.

"I'll do it though, *if* it's not for me. If you'll allow me to help others in order to help myself—to save others so I can save myself. And if you'll make sure I have a place to live, with a roof over my head, and if you'll give me peace of mind, I will walk with you. I will walk away from everything that is demonic or perverted or evil."

Without even realizing it, I had just volunteered for the exact same type of mission that Jesus sent Tomb Man on— a mission to the downtrodden and those who had known him before, in his demon-possessed state.

I somehow sensed that everything I had been through in the first fifty years of my life was intended to prepare me to bring hope to the hopeless, to teach the downcast to look up, and to show others the way out of their brokenness and addiction.

All I had to do was overcome my own addiction.

It's not like I made a promise to God that I'd clean up my act and instantly all the cravings for that next hit were gone. Not by any stretch.

Emotionally and mentally drained and physically exhausted, I lay back down into the garbage, staring at the ceiling, wondering what was next.

Eventually I fell asleep.

When I awoke, something was different. I could sense it, but I couldn't think what it was.

Then it came back to me.

I had promised God that I was going to finally clean up my act for real and stay clean and help others to get their lives in order as well.

Could I really do that?

Well, I'd made a promise. I'd have to give it my best shot.

I dragged myself to my feet and looked around the room at the bloody, smelly mess I had made of the place. Pornography and drug paraphernalia were everywhere. Demonic drawings from my own hand plastered the walls.

The room encapsulated the low to which I had fallen.

If I was to climb out of the hole, come out of my tomb, and not only face the light of day but bring light to others, I would have to begin by removing the darkness from my own life.

Most of the windows in my two rooms no longer had glass in them, so I had covered them with cardboard and old curtains and blinds. I lived in a dark world, a tomb of my own making.

I went to a window and threw open the curtains. The light streaming in hurt my eyes, but I needed it. Needed to have it show me what my life had become.

It was shocking to behold in the full light of day.

In a frenzy I began to tear posters and drawings off the walls and stuff them into garbage bags.

On my hands and knees I began to pick up slivers of glass and baggies that had brought my chosen poisons into my life.

I scoured both my rooms, picking up drugs, paraphernalia, pornography, occult materials, and trash. I filled bags with refuse that I was determined to remove from my life.

I cleaned myself up as best I could in the bathroom, then as darkness descended on the streets, I went out. My mission this night was far different from any before. I carried bag after bag of my former life to various dumpsters, scattering the remnants of my past from place to place in hopes that no one would pick up the pieces and fall into the pit I knew I needed to dig my way out of.

The task completed, I lay down on my bed, determined to sleep rather than prowl through the night.

When I woke up the next morning, I felt different. I knew something drastic had changed in my life, but I wasn't sure what it was.

Then as I looked around the room, I realized what I had done.

There was not a pipe or bong or baggie anywhere to be seen.

Had I really thrown it all away?

"You answered the call," the quiet voice reminded me.

No! Surely not! There must be something here. What sort of stupid, crazy idea had gotten into my head? Did I really think I could live without my drugs? I had tried so many times and failed. What was the point of even trying anymore? Just give me my hit! Let me escape the world, fly into euphoria, be free of myself, my pain, my guilt!

As frantically as I had cleaned the place the day before, I now scoured it in search of some last scrap that could carry me back to my familiar, dark world.

But there was nothing.

I sat down on the edge of my bed, despair tearing at my insides. I'm nothing but a dope fiend. I can't do this! Who did I think I was, to think that I could escape the darkness? I was Nico the Dragon, the very personification of all the evil in the world. There was no changing that. I needed drugs, and I needed them now!

Then there was a knock on my door.

Who could it be?

No one dared come to the Dragon's Lair uninvited.

I sat, staring at the door, seeing it as a portal to my destiny.

Whatever or whoever was on the other side would decide my fate.

I got up off the bed and walked slowly, expectantly to the door, unfastened one chain, then another, turned one lock, then another, and finally turned the knob and opened the portal to whatever my future held.

"Need a hit, Dragon?"

It was my dealer.

"Remember your promise," the quiet voice in my head said.

"Yeah, yeah man, you're just in time, I got the cash right here, just hold on a sec."

I found my wallet and pulled out $200 and hurried to the door, my hands shaking with anticipation. He took the money, then said "I gotta go across town to get it."

"What man, you don't got it on you?" I narrowed my eyes as I looked at him. "Well, I'll just write you a check for it then. Careful not to drop it though, it'll bounce up and break your nose!"

"It's just across town. Take me twenty minutes to get it. You can come with me. We can take your car. Twenty minutes, that's all it'll take."

My heart was beating fast with anticipation. I was about to be delivered from my pain. And now this?

I grabbed the money out of his hand and glared at him. "When it's in your pocket, let me know!"

"Come on, Dragon, you know you need it."

"Just forget it, man. I'm done." I hung my head, shut the door, and turned and began to pace back and forth across my room, to the window, back to the door. What should I do? I could go out on the street and have drugs. An eight-ball a day keeps everyone but the demons away.

"Remember your promise."

I sat down, staring at the floor, my hands locked together to try to stop their shaking, perspiration dripping from my brow. I wanted it, I needed it, I could taste it.

"Remember your promise."

"Why won't you leave me alone?" I shouted, trying to drown out that quiet voice.

"Remember your promise."

I was paralyzed, torn between two destinies. Every physical fiber of my body screamed for just one more hit. But my mind said I had had enough of that. It cried out for a sense of peace.

The tug-of-war raged inside me for half an hour or more. One minute I was ready to jump up and run to the street, the next I was physically restraining myself by clinging for dear life to the seat of my chair.

I couldn't imagine right and good triumphing in this battle.

I couldn't envision my life as anything but a dope fiend, living minute-to-minute in anticipation of his next fix.

But I was a fighter. I knew what it meant to go up against powerful odds and enemies. And so the two powers continued to go at each other. No holds barred. Going for total domination and submission.

Words I had heard before began to play in my mind.

Will we ever come to understand
On this path of destruction that the end of all man
Is the last stop? It doesn't matter the stories of how we came
Does the ending always have to turn out to be the same?
When those city blocks of those sidewalks begin calling out
our name.

So I will keep asking only for your answer,
One right now we desperately need.
Can we find peace of mind, keep our hope alive?
For we are all trying to survive.
What's left for us to believe in?

Why would someone as perfect as you,
The creator of everyone and everything,
Lord of Lords and King above all Kings,
Why would you take the time to listen
To a broken lost confused addicted sinner like me?

The words I heard posed a question I could not answer. Why would God have any interest in me? Had I just imagined he cared enough to speak to me? But still, where did the words come from? The words that spoke to my soul, and to the souls of countless others among the downcast, debauched, distraught and lost.

The words were calling to me. But so was something else.

Knock … knock … knock.

Who could it be this time?

At least it gave me something to focus on other than the battle inside.

I got up from my chair and went to the door.

My dealer was back, and this time he had the drugs in his hand, ready to make the sale.

"You told me to come back when I had it in my pocket." He looked down at the baggie. "Well, here it is Dragon. What you need."

The battle raged inside me. I opened my mouth, but no words came out. I stared at him, my head slightly moving from side to side.

"Come on Dragon, man. I went clear cross town for you!"

Still I just stared at him without making a move.

"Listen man, I laid out cold, hard cash for you, now you better pony up!" His shoulder began to lean in on me, his brow creased, his tones threatening.

He'd never tried that kind of thing on me before. People like him always had friends of the kind that would make anyone's life who didn't pay their bills really painful. It didn't matter how tough you were, if someone hit you from behind with a baseball bat when you weren't looking.

Up to that time we had coexisted in a relationship of supplier and customer, showing mutual respect. Now he was moving in on me, trying to force me to buy, and it shook me out of my trance. I resented him and his attitude. Nobody told Nico the Dragon what he had to do!

Now I had an opponent outside myself to deal with. I knew which side I had to come down on. "What do I do?" I asked myself. "Do I hurt him?"

The voice that had been speaking to me answered. "Nah, he's hurt enough already."

The dealer always wore dark glasses—like he thought that kept people from knowing what he really looked like. I reached out slowly to him and pulled his shades off, and looked right into his eyes. "I know who you are."

I paused, relishing the tension I saw in his eyes.

"I know why you're here."

He nodded slightly, looking like he wanted to be on agreeable terms with me, but at the same time inched backwards to run if he had to.

"And you know what, man? I appreciate that you came at me that way. Because now I know whose side you're on. So I need you to listen very carefully to what I'm going to say."

He swallowed hard and took a quick glance down the stairs toward the street.

"Look at me, man!"

His eyes met mine, but they were surrendered, fearful eyes.

"I don't need them. I don't want them. I'm done. And I never want to see you around this place again."

"Okay man, okay man, I hear you bro'. No offense man, I'm gone. You know where to find me, anything changes, yeah?"

"Wait," I said, and I pulled a $20 bill out of my pocket. "Here's twenty bucks for your trouble. You can get yourself a sandwich, you can get yourself whatever you need. I hope you don't go get drugs with it, but if you do, you do. And hey, it's kind of cold out there. You need a jacket? Here, take mine." I handed him a spare jacket I'd found while cleaning up the place.

He just stared at me, didn't seem to know how to react, so I pushed his shades back onto his face then closed the door. A moment later I heard him go down the steps. He never knocked on my door again.

Chapter 16

My decision had been made, and a drug pusher had helped me make it by pushing too hard. I had seen the devil in his face, and though a day earlier I had wanted to spit in Satan's eye and die; now I wanted to live.

When you have been on an extended meth high, the pain of coming down is intense, raging through your body like an electrical storm. The pain I endured over the next several days was far worse than anything I had suffered in any boxing ring, MMA match, or street fight, and it just went on and on. Many were the times I told myself it just wasn't worth it—that all I needed to do to escape the torture was to take another hit.

I had the money, I had the contacts. Getting another few grams of meth would be easier than going out for a quart of milk.

But every time I got up off my bed of pain to go do the deed, that quiet voice would speak up again. "Remember your promise," and somehow I would stop myself.

If you've never experienced addiction, you can't understand how hard that was. It was hardest battle of my life. But I sensed that there were now powers pulling upward, just like there had been demons pushing me into the abyss.

Still, I felt like I was just one breath from death. My energy for years had all come from chemical stimulation, now it was a struggle just to wake up and get up. For days I did little but sleep and suffer. Pain had been part of my life for so long that what I felt now was nothing new, but the problem was that I knew I could make it go away with drugs. That was a powerful, powerful temptation and motivation to fall.

Gradually my mind began to clear of all the pain, and I began to be able to see through the haze into the future.

That was troubling.

I hadn't thought seriously about my future for an eternity. I had always lived life full throttle with no regard for consequences or where I was headed. For the past year the only thing I'd seen in my future was a grave.

Now I'd made a promise to God: If you'll let me save others in order to save myself, I'll walk away from all these demons, drugs, and evil.

Walking away from evil was one thing. But where was I supposed to walk *to?*

And how was I supposed to save others?

I was barely functional myself. In those lost years I had lost so much. I had to learn all over again how to brush my teeth and my hair. Nico the Dragon, who had once taken such pride in his appearance, had lost all sense of self-respect, and he looked like it.

I could barely speak a coherent sentence; words came out in stammers and stutters except when I was reciting a Spoken Word.

The side effects of meth addiction include paranoia and panic attacks. I had always thought of myself as the tough, invincible guardian of my neighborhood, afraid of no one and no thing. Now, as my mind tried to recover from years of overstimulation, I was afraid of my own shadow. Afraid that danger lurked behind every door and window. I could barely make myself go out on the street. If I went into a store to buy food, I would sometimes end up dropping my shopping basket in the aisle and almost running out the door, fearful of some little child who was staring at me, or even just the cry of a baby.

But I couldn't let myself keep hiding in my room for

long. There was another crisis brewing. The company that had purchased the apartment building from the bank was ready to start renovations. Everybody had to move out.

Where could I go?

I remembered that my promise to God had included a caveat: If you'll provide me with a place to live—a roof over my head—I'll walk away from evil.

Well, now the roof was being taken away.

Did that mean I didn't have to live up to my end of the bargain?

It would make a good excuse to go back to my old ways, and the way I was feeling these days, I didn't need much of an excuse.

As I sat in my room one day, paralyzed by fear of the future, wondering where I would go, how I would survive on the mean streets, someone knocked on my door.

I stared at the door from across the room, afraid even to ask who was there, hoping they would just go away and leave me alone.

Knock, Knock, Knock, Knock, Knock. It was louder. The police? No, not this, now? I don't need this! An old friend had recently given me a large stash of marijuana in payment of a debt, and it was there with me. I hadn't touched it, but if the police found it, I'd be on my way to jail. Maybe that was where I was supposed to go to try to save others? At least I'd have a roof over my head.

No! I don't want that. Not now!

Pound! Pound! Pound! They weren't knocking anymore. "Dragon—come to the door. I know you're in there. Open up, bro."

Johnny? Could it really be Johnny? I hadn't seen him in weeks, but he lived just down the street and operated a legal medical marijuana shop. I also knew he was a meth addict and probably sold it on the side as well.

Well, there's your answer. He probably has an eight-ball in his pocket. He'd be glad to trade it for the weed I'm sitting on. Never mind that it wouldn't solve the problem of a place to live. The meth would make my worries go away.

"Come on, Dragon. I need to talk to you."

A battle royal raged within me as I stood and shuffled toward the door.

"Johnny—that you?"

"You know it is, Dragon, come on, let me in."

My shaking hands fumbled with the chain locks. When I finally got the door open, my whole body was trembling. Tension, fear, and anticipation all shook me.

"Hey bro, you all right? Can I come in?" he said after several seconds had passed and I hadn't spoken.

I stepped aside and he walked in and stood in the middle of the room, looking around. My few possessions were stashed in cardboard boxes and plastic bags. Move-out day was less than a week away.

"So I hear you're gettin' the boot. Where you gonna land, Dragon?"

"I uh, I've got some friends..."

"Look man, word on the street is you're clean. That straight up?"

"I uh, yeah, man. I'm not using anymore."

He walked around me, looking me over like a car shopper ready to kick the tires. "Yeah, I seen you out and about, other day. You're different, man. You look better. That's good. That's cool, man. I'm happy for you."

I half nodded, wondering what he was getting at. I thought of him as a drug dealer, and drug dealers never, ever congratulate someone on getting clean. Insult you, curse you, try to drive you back down into your hole of dependency, yes. But congratulate you? Encourage you? Never.

"So these friends o' yours. They close?"

"What friends?"

"Where you're kickin' back, man. Where you're puttin' down, layin' your ugly head."

"Yeah, they're not too far," I lied.

"Close in like, Hollywood, Echo Park, Silver Lake?"

"I dunno, exactly."

"You got nothin', right man? Come on, shoot straight

with me Dragon. I seen you around. Heard about you. You're tryna get straight, and I'm cool with that. It's righteous man, a good thing."

"Yeah. I heard this voice—I mean I made this promise, Johnny. Like I was talking to God or something. He said he wants me to save other people, and that's how he'll save me."

"I don't believe in God, but whatever's clever. You need a spot or not?"

"I thought you wanted to sell me some..."

"Nah, man. That's not what I'm here about. I heard about you. You're a big guy, tough guy. Just the kinda guy it's good to have on these streets, keep the lowlife in check, you know what I'm hittin' at. Don't wanna see you leave, see your sorry ass out on the streets. Come on over to my place. Got a spare room right in front, we'll let you have it."

"You don't understand, man. I gotta get away from this scene. Gotta get my life back in order. I can't be around that stuff you're doin'."

"You misinterpret my intentions, man. I ain't offerin' you no hits, no dope, no Mary Jane, no nothin' except a place to lay your ugly head and you watch my back and I'll watch yours, you just gotta stay clean. You can't touch the stuff, you can't smoke the stuff. You can't snort the stuff. You can't shoot the stuff. You can't eat it, you can't drink it, you can't even touch it. Not even weed, man. You do an' you're out just like that. I don't need no fiend leechin' off me. Come on over. Tomorrow. We'll have the place ready for you. Free room. Really man, we need you 'round here Dragon."

It took several minutes for him to convince me. Nobody, no drug dealer, ever made an offer like that. Only reason they'd normally let you in was to sell to you, get you hooked, make you dependent. Now he wanted me to move into his house on the condition I *wouldn't* buy from him. Was God already working in my life? Working miracles?

*So don't smoke that H, drop that E or toke that Cush or Mary
Jane
Don't race around with the new one on the block
Because the label always reads the same.
Quick to accuse, certain to abuse, and you never stick around
to accept any pain
Over and over and over again.
Rock bottom starts the day that you got 'em.*

Chapter 17

Still hardly believing that he wanted me around as anything but a customer, I moved into Johnny's place on Oakwood Avenue. He and his current live-in girlfriend moved to the back of the house, giving me the front bedroom where it would be easy for me to keep an eye on goings and comings.

All I had to do was be there, which was about all I was capable of anyhow.

My brain and body had undergone so much abuse for so long that it would take many months for me to recover to the point where I could become anything more than a ghost, lurking around the edges of civilized society.

So, if Jesus cast the demons out of Tomb Man and just that quick he was clothed and in his right mind, why couldn't he do the same for me?

I don't mean to imply that I fully understand the mind of God, but I think I can understand why that didn't happen.

I couldn't be trusted with it.

If I had been instantly restored, back to the man I was before I set out to destroy myself, I wouldn't have learned a thing by the experience. I probably would have fallen right back into my old ways, reasoning that my folly had no consequences. "I can quit anytime and be back to normal instantly," I would have told myself.

And that would have been the end of me. I had tried to quit many times before, but always relapsed. Now, though,

I had my promise to cling to, and that quiet voice that kept reminding me of it.

The paranoia and self-loathing that had led me into addiction, and that had been fed by my drug use, did not evaporate. I will probably be suffering some of the consequences of my mistakes for as long as I live, and that is part of the message I share with the young people I mentor these days. I want them to understand that getting started on drugs, even in a small way, is risking their whole future.

I lived in Johnny's house for several months, just existing for the most part, I suppose. Whenever I could get up my courage to go out, I would cruise the streets of the familiar neighborhood, stopping and talking with people— especially those who looked like they were really down. The Spoken Word continued to develop in me during those days, and I'd often share a message that I felt impressed might help the person I was talking to.

I felt like maybe I was doing some good for the world, but a deep sense of frustration haunted me. I was still very angry at the world in general, and at myself in particular. Since I was living at Johnny's as an invited guest, I knew I needed to treat the place respectfully. At my own place when I'd get angry, I'd often punch my fist through the plaster walls or head-butt the wall. I couldn't do that as a guest. But people would sometimes see me on the street head-butting a power pole or some other solid object.

The next day they might see me urgently sharing The Spoken Word with a derelict in the gutter.

I didn't feel like I was making any real progress. Was talking to people too spaced-out to respond rationally really all that my ministry—my saving others so I could save myself—was supposed to accomplish? Often I'd feel so frustrated that I would start punching myself in the face again.

"Is this all you got for me, God?" I asked one day. Somehow I sensed that it was God who had called me, even though I knew very little about him, and didn't know where to turn to learn to know him better. "I can't go on like this forever. Did you really call me as your witness, or is it all in my head? I need some sort of sign..."

Later that day Eddie, who had shared my previous apartment, came by with a friend I'll call Ricardo.

Eddie looked really disheveled, like he'd probably been living on the streets ever since we lost our apartment. Ricardo was a gang-banger of the type that's called a shot-caller on the streets—a big, rough-looking guy who I assumed never went out without a pistol in his pocket. When his gang needed some enforcement work done, or if they wanted to intimidate someone, he was their man.

"Hey Dragon, you're lookin' good—how you doin'?" Eddie said.

I'd seen him around some, because he sometimes worked for Johnny, doing marijuana deliveries and recruiting new customers. So he was around pretty regularly. I hadn't seen Ricardo with him before, though.

"How's it hangin', my man?" I greeted Eddie, then looked at Ricardo. I figured I'd better keep an eye on him, for security reasons.

Eddie and I exchanged pleasantries and good-natured jibes for a bit, then he said that Ricardo wanted to talk to me.

"What's up, my man?" I reached out and we did a quick hand clasp.

"Nothin' I'm just lookin' to kill me a few niggers today." By using the N word he wasn't referring to people of any particular race or skin color, but to whoever it was that he thought, or had been told, deserved to die.

I glanced at Eddie, who shrugged, then back to Ricardo. "Yeah?"

"So I heard you got this Spoken Word or somethin'. What's that all about, man?"

"I am so honored to say that I am just one of the many of God's soldiers," I began to recite to him, from the start of a Spoken Word I had just completed. "And just like every one of you, I am involved in a fierce battle."

I went on reciting for him, and the rhythm of the poetry and its message seemed almost to entrance him.

"That's really sweet, man," he said when I finished. "Where'd you get that anyhow?"

"It's a gift, Bro. Those aren't my words. They're for you, though. And anybody else who will listen."

"Yeah, right," he said. "Come on, let's bounce," he said to Eddie. "I got me some fools to kill." He seemed really agitated.

I didn't know whether he had a gun or not, or whether he was serious about wanting to kill someone that day, so I launched into another Spoken Word, hoping the words would somehow calm him. When I finished, he just looked at me and said, "Yeah, okay man. Cool for you, but not my school, got it? I gotta go."

"Hey, thanks man," Eddie said. "You really got something there. Keep it up."

Ricardo was already in the driveway, heading for the street. Eddie hurried to catch up with him, and I followed him out the door to the street and watched the two of them go.

When they were just about out of sight, there was a loud Bang Bang Bang! That wasn't firecrackers. I knew the sound of a pistol when I heard it, and I thought at first that I must be one of the "niggers" that Ricardo wanted to kill that day. I didn't even duck. I guess I thought maybe this was God's answer to my questions: No, I wasn't really doing any good, so I might as well die.

But no bullets hit me. There were people all up and down the street, but I didn't see anyone fall to the ground. What had just happened? I wasn't about to go running after them to find out—that would be suicidal.

Eddie came by later and told me that Ricardo had pulled a pistol out of his pocket and pointed it at him. From the look in Ricardo's eyes, Eddie was sure he was about to die. But then, for no reason, Ricardo pointed the gun at the sky and fired off several rounds. "Then we both took off running. He went one way and I went the other."

Ricardo's reaction, after hearing The Spoken Word, provided an answer for me. Perhaps I really had saved someone's life that day, by sharing the gift that had been given to me. With that little bit of encouragement, I could keep on trying to live the life I thought God had called me to.

I stayed on at Johnny's for several more months, but it wasn't a great environment for me. Johnny and his girlfriend were using meth, and one time I found a pipe with crystals in it stashed away. I picked it up and looked at it. It seemed to be speaking to me. "Just one. Think how good it will feel." Every fiber of my body craved *just one* hit. I rolled the pipe between my fingers. It felt like coming home. I started to put it to my lips, looking around for a lighter to heat it with.

But then there was that pesky voice. "Remember your promise." Why couldn't I shut it off? I laid the pipe on a table and stood staring at it, turning away, but then feeling it pull my eyes back. My mouth watered, thinking of how it would feel to inhale those vapors again, for the first time in months.

"Rock bottom starts the day you got 'em" the phrase from one of the Spoken Words poems I had been given interposed itself, and the message I had been trying to communicate to others came back to me.

I opened that door, I walked on in,
That's when Satan, the addiction, the darkness started to begin.
So I opened up my heart, I let God's Spirit in.
That's when that addiction came to an end.

So don't ever party like me.
The truth is I used to start at OD,
Busy watching Intervention on TV,
Living the lie my life could be so carefree.

I made it through the day, but would I live to see the night?
I'm tripping in the darkness, and I can't see the light.
I'm living in the high, I'm so cool for the while.
I'm the judge and I'm the jury, and I'm at my own trial.

But the verdict is in, and it read guilty as sin.
And there's laughter, but there isn't a smile.

Rock bottom starts the day you got 'em.
You think about your family, but the truth is you forgot 'em.
I think about my enemy, but I ain't never fought him.
The true enemy lives inside of me.
I give you that for free, see?
Please don't ever get high,
'Cause all them evil spirits man, they tryna see you die.

My hands shaking, I picked up a napkin off the table, then picked up the pipe and wrapped it in the napkin, then laid it on the floor and put my heel on it and smashed it to bits.

I had come within inches of falling back into my old ways.

I wish I could say it felt really good to smash that pipe. The truth is I was full of questions, almost regretting what I had done. My life didn't seem to be moving forward. I still found it extremely difficult to go out in public. I was living on welfare checks, hunkering down in a place I didn't have to pay for. My life seemed to be the complete opposite of what it had once been, and I couldn't see any way to get back to anything like normal. The world I lived in was dark, and I could only see darkness in my future.

Not long after that the house I was living in was foreclosed and sold to new owners. Now I wasn't sure I'd even have a roof over my head in my bleak future. But a friend helped me find a place not far away in North Hollywood, where I could rent two rooms in a house owned by an octogenarian atheist of all things.

Well, maybe that would be my opportunity to save someone else. Maybe the words I was being given would speak to my landlord and help him give his life to God? Maybe my life could get out of neutral and start to move forward again.

Chapter 18

Things didn't turn out the way I had hoped in my new digs. I rented one room in a house and kept my cat Squeaky in another room. The landlord lived in a guest house at the back of the property. I had been given a cash payout from the new owners when I moved out of Johnny's place, so I at least had a bit of money for rent.

But now I found myself being even more isolated than at Johnny's place, and I felt myself sinking back into the darkness. The world outside was far too familiar to me. Strip clubs where I'd spent many a night partying were just down the street. People who had supplied me with drugs were still hawking their wares in the shadows. I didn't feel safe going out—there were too many opportunities to fall back into my old life.

As I retreated deeper and deeper into my shell, I concentrated on the words I had been reciting, and from time to time I'd go to the back house and try to share them with Alf, my octogenarian atheist landlord. He didn't appreciate it; he seemed bent on persuading me that I was just hallucinating, and that there was no god who had spoken to me, and I might as well give up on trying to save myself or anyone else.

Cali, a stripper I'd partied with in the past, soon found out I was back in the neighborhood and buttonholed me one day when I was out of my lair. "Hey Dragon, why don't you have me over some night for a little party? Remember the fun we used to have? You know I can show you a really good time?"

Well, maybe this was somebody I was supposed to try to save—maybe I should have her over, I rationalized, and share the Spoken Word with her, so I agreed.

As the time for her arrival came near, I began to feel conflicted.

I knew what "party" meant in her lingo.

She would be bringing some crystals with her. She would want us to get high and see where the spirits took us. It was a scene I'd played a thousand times, and it was inviting, comforting, familiar. I wasn't getting anywhere good, anyhow. Why not just go back to the old ways? What harm was there in it? Life was too difficult. Why not party hearty, then die?

As the minutes ticked down to when Cali would waltz back into my life and start me down that dark path, I could feel two destinies wrestling inside me. Retreat into the familiar had the advantage. It pointed me to a well-traveled, downhill path to a destination I did not fear.

The invitation to look up seemed to offer only questions—a steep, crooked path leading into a bank of fog, an uncertain destiny, and no easy answers.

I tried to put all of that out of my mind, to focus on how much fun it would be to spend the night with Cali and the stuff she would bring with her to fuel our party.

Whatever happened in the next hour would determine whether I remained true to my promise or not.

Finally, with trembling hands, I picked up my phone and called her number. "Yeah, Cali. Something's come up. It's not gonna work out for tonight. Maybe another time."

"You sure Dragon, I got some really good—"

"Not tonight, Cali. I got other things I gotta do."

"Damn, Dragon, I really wanna see you. Can't we just..."

I pulled the phone away from my ear as she resorted to her pouty voice, and pressed the disconnect button.

I had come within minutes of going back on my promise, and it scared me. Every time I went out on the street, it was as if the familiar places where I'd wasted so much of my life were calling to me, inviting me in. It was only about eight months since I'd quit using drugs, and as the year wound down and the days got shorter and nights longer, the temptation to slide back to my old ways grew stronger and stronger.

I had to get out of there if I was serious about taking the upward path.

But where could I go?

I thought about a close friend who has a big house in Malibu. My dad and his dad considered themselves brothers, even though they weren't related, so Eric and I called ourselves cousins.

Back in the day when I was riding high, going to movie premieres and strutting my stuff around Hollywood, Eric had been a big fan, and had sometimes accompanied me to events and parties, enjoying sharing the access my connections got me.

He had watched in dismay as I descended into my private hell, and had eventually cut off contact. No doubt partly because most times when I called him I would start hinting for a handout or loan, and he knew what I would do with any money that came my way.

Somehow I had managed to keep a cell phone through all my years of wild living, and I still had Eric's number in it. Should I call him? What would I say? He was all-too-familiar with how often I had tried to get my life together, only to fall back into old habits.

But I needed a change of environment, so I made the call.

Eric listened to my story, and when I mentioned I needed a place to stay, instead of turning me down outright, he asked how long I'd been clean.

"About a year and a half," I lied.

"I need some time to think about it, my man," he said. "I'll talk to my wife and daughters and get back to you."

In Hollywood "I'll get back to you" is just a roundabout way of saying *No*, so I didn't think I would be hearing from

Eric anytime soon. But he surprised me. A couple days later he was on the phone saying that they had a spare bedroom in their beautiful home, and that I was welcome to come and stay with them for a while, see how it would work out. I found out later that a lot of times when a Christian says "I'll get back to you," it means they feel the need to pray about an answer before responding. That's what Eric did, he prayed about it and talked to his family, and together they agreed to give me a chance.

And what a life-changing chance that turned out to be! None of us could have imagined or dreamed how much impact that one simple decision would have, not only on my life, but on many others' lives as well.

Chapter 19

I had felt the need of a change of scenery, and boy did I get one! From living in a dumpy little house in a run-down section of North Hollywood, with strip clubs and XXX-rated book stores just down the street, I moved to a big, comfortable house in the hills above beautiful Malibu, with A-list movie stars for neighbors.

Eric and his family were amazing in their willingness to welcome his long-lost friend into their home, despite all they knew about me. They gave me my own room, which had been set up as an apartment with a refrigerator and bathroom. And their welcoming me in eventually led to the doors being opened for me to enter the next phase of the ministry that God was calling me to.

I was far from ready for that type of ministry though, when I moved into their beautiful home.

Theirs was a vibrant, active Christian family. Their two teenage daughters were constantly coming and going to school and events and having friends over. That amount of activity around me made me nervous. I still wasn't ready to integrate back into a social life, so I spent most of my time isolated in my private room.

Of course I needed to go out for groceries from time to time, and even that was a huge crisis for me. Eric's home was in the country, and it was a six-mile drive to get to a supermarket. By time I was at the store, I could barely make myself get out of the car and go in, and once I was inside, the number of choices overwhelmed me. I was used to going to the 99-cent store and buying whatever food was there. A huge supermarket was more than I could handle. Several times I had to leave the store in a panic without getting what I had come for.

That made me even more frustrated, and I would take it out on myself. I began hitting myself in the face again. Eric saw me do that one time, and that worried him. To make matters worse, it turned out that both his daughters were allergic to cats, and I had of course moved Squeaky in with me.

As gracious as they were, by early December—ten months after I'd quit doing drugs—it was becoming apparent that I would soon need to find another place to live.

"Come to church with us tomorrow," Eric suggested one day.

Being around a whole bunch of strangers was not my idea of a fun adventure, but how could I turn him down, after all he had done for me? "Okay," I said hesitantly.

The following morning found us walking through the garden-like grounds of the Thousand Oaks Seventh-day Adventist Church on our way to the entrance.

The church has a little plaza in front of its doors, where pastoral staff and others greet those who are coming to services.

As we entered that area, a large man in a nice suit singled me out and came up to talk to me. Maybe it was because of the way I was dressed—all in black. I'm sure I looked a bit different from most of the people coming to church.

He reached out to shake my hand "Hello, I don't believe we've met. I just want to welcome you to our church."

I shook his hand. "Have you attended here before?" he asked.

"I haven't been to church in a long time," I confessed.

"Well, we want you to feel really welcome here! By the way I'm Pastor Meager," he said, still clasping my hand.

"Nice to meet you, I'm Nico."

"Well Nico, what brings you here? Tell me a little about yourself."

I couldn't believe that the pastor of the congregation was taking the time to stop and talk with someone like me, but there was something about him that made me feel comfortable opening up. I began sharing my story with him, telling him how I felt God had delivered me from addiction and given me special messages that were intended to bring hope into others' lives.

He listened intently, asking questions, showing a real interest not only in my story, but in me as a person. "That's amazing, Nico," he said after several minutes. "You know what? I sense that God has called you to a very special ministry, and that he is going to open the doors for you to minister to a group of people the church can't usually reach."

"Really? You think so?"

"There's something special happening here, Nico. I really believe God has sent you here today so we could meet, because he wanted me to encourage you to keep on pursuing opportunities for ministry."

"What would you suggest I do, Pastor?" I asked, intrigued.

"Would you be willing to come back to church next week and share your testimony with the congregation?"

There must have been a look of terror in my eyes, because he smiled and put his hand on my shoulder. "Just think about it. Let me know. We'll have a spot for you in the service—I think God is calling you."

"I'll do it, Pastor." I know the courage to say that didn't come from anywhere inside of me, the guy who froze up when he tried to exchange pleasantries with the cashier at the grocery store.

That visit on the church patio turned out to be a major turning point in my new life.

I spoke at the church the following week, and after the service Pastor Meager and many members of the congregation came to me to affirm me in ministry and ask if I'd speak again the following week, which I did.

I didn't know it at the time, but the pastor was so deeply impressed that God had called me to minister to a group of people the church wouldn't otherwise be able to reach that he started checking into my background and talking to church leaders about me. "We need to find a way to help this man get involved in ministry," he told them.

It was about this time that Eric came to me and told me that it just wasn't working out for me to live with his family. He could see that I still had a long ways to go to where I could be comfortable around people, so he asked if there wasn't someplace else I could go, other than back to Hollywood where friends had offered me a room that looked more like a dungeon than a bedroom.

"I just don't know," I said.

"What about your dad?"

"He wouldn't take me. I tried that a few years ago, and he told me I wasn't welcome at his place." I had asked him to let me live with him for a bit when I was unemployed and headed down the wrong path, and he'd told me my life had been like a meteor, and that I was about to burn out, and he didn't want to see it happen, so I was on my own. Not welcome.

"But it's different now, isn't it? I'd be willing to talk to him, tell him how you've changed." I could see deep compassion and concern in Eric's eyes as he looked at me.

"I guess we could try."

When I made the call, I was surprised that my father, who I hadn't lived with for nearly forty years, said yes, I could come stay with him and his wife in Corona for a while.

I didn't want to stay there for long, but I didn't have a plan for where I would go from there, either. Dad welcomed me and gave me, and my cat Squeaky, a room in their mobile home, which was located in a nice facility with a swimming pool and gym. Because Squeaky is a feral cat that wasn't socialized with humans as a kitten, she is even less comfortable around people than I was at that stage of my life. I'm the only person she responds positively to; strangers are more likely to get a hiss and growl than a purr from her. So, wherever I lived, she had to either live in my room or have another room to call her own. She couldn't be out with the other residents.

I moved in with Dad, who is in his late 70s, and his wife, who is closer to my age, in early 2012. When Pastor Meager heard that I would be moving about 100 miles away, he was very concerned for me. "God has called you to a very special ministry, Nico," he said. "Let's keep in contact and see what God has in store for you."

It's amazing to me to consider how much concern he showed for me, someone he'd only barely gotten acquainted with. But he told me that God had spoken to his heart, telling him not to let this man go—that God had a special mission for me, to reach people that the church normally would not be able to reach.

About the middle of January, Pastor Meager called me up and told me he wanted to talk to me about a special opportunity. He said some people at the church had put up the money to make it possible for me to go get some training in evangelism and Bible study.

He had gone to the church elders and challenged them, "If we really want to be what a church should be, we need to help Nico. We need to get him some training and experience, get him grounded in the church, so that he can fulfill the mission I believe God has called him to."

The church had stepped up and put up the money, so now he was challenging me. "It's a four-month evangelistic training program at a place called AFCOE in northern California. These people have donated several thousand dollars to support you in this, because they believe in you and the mission God has called you to, Nico. So, what do you say? Will you go?"

I didn't commit right away, but a few days later I agreed to at least give it a try. Pastor Meager drove all the way over to my folks' place and picked me up and took me back to the church, where there was some sort of social event going on.

He wanted me to come in and fellowship with the people, but I still wasn't at all comfortable in large groups, so I told him I wanted to just sit in the car and think and pray about it, that I still wasn't sure that I wanted to go to AFCOE.

"I understand your hesitation," he said. "It's a big step. You need to pray about it and be sure God is blessing in this, but I'll tell you this, the people of the church have already prayed about it a lot, and they've put up the money to give you this chance. Opportunities like this are few and far between in life."

"I know."

"You'll really consider it, then, won't you?"

"Sure." I doubt that I sounded very sure.

He left me there in the parking lot while he went into the fellowship hall. As I sat there in his car, looking around at the flowers and trees, my old fears came back to haunt me. I thought I could see demons hiding in the bushes. In my mind's eye I saw the pastor's face shape-shift, turning into a demon. I shook my head, chasing those images away, but I couldn't shake the feeling of dread. If I went so far away, I sensed that I would never come back—I was being set up; this would be the end of me. I just couldn't do it. My paranoia was running full-force.

Pastor M. came back about the time I decided I wouldn't go. "Well, what do you think?" he asked.

"I can't do it. I just can't do it. I don't want to be in debt to the people who put up the money. It's just not right for me. I'm not ready for it."

He sat down beside me there in the car, and there were tears in his eyes. "Are you sure, Nico? I believe God has called you, and this will enable you..."

"I just can't do it, Pastor. It's not right for me."

He sat quietly for a few minutes, then tried one more time. "I respect your answer. I don't want to push you into something you're not ready for. But at the same time, I believe God has put this plan together for you, because of the way he is going to use you to reach people that this congregation could never touch. That's why the people are behind you—they don't expect to be paid back. This is a gift, Nico."

All I could do was shake my head. I just wasn't catching the same vision he was.

"Do this for me, will you? Before you give me your final answer. Just take a walk around the grounds, ask the Lord one more time whether he will empower you to do this. Will you do that for me, Nico?"

I couldn't say no to the man who had done so much for me, so I got out and walked through the gardens surrounding the church. As I passed the fellowship hall, I saw groups of people, all dressed very conservatively, standing around talking, good-naturedly teasing, and doing what Christians call "fellowshipping." It made my skin crawl. I couldn't possibly go join in with them.

I envisioned myself going to a school where everybody was like that, or probably even more even-tempered and conservative. The contrast with the life I was accustomed to was stark. I could not envision myself ever fitting into a group like that.

I wandered on, and eventually found a secluded spot where I could sit and pray. "What do you want me to do, God? What do you want me to do? Is this really your plan for me?"

It was a warm, clear January day in Southern California, not a breeze was moving as I began to recite one of my Spoken Words, looking for answers, looking up into the heavens, waiting to hear God's voice.

Just then the wind began to stir the leaves overhead, then a refreshing wave of cool air ascended from the ravine behind the church. Was that God's Spirit moving?

I looked down into the flower garden at my feet and saw something I hadn't noticed before—an old Bible. I picked it up. It was soaking wet, its pages wrinkled, like it had been underwater for a hundred years.

My troubled, trembling mind couldn't make out a reason why it should be wet while everything else was dry. Was this some sort of sign? If so, what did it mean?

Don't' get me wrong, I don't think that every oddity we encounter in life is some sort of supernatural communication to us. But in that setting, as I wrestled with what I realized was a life-changing dilemma, the wet Bible brought me up short.

"God, if you really want me to go, I'll go. But what about Squeaky?" My dad and step mom had agreed to take care of her. "But what if they leave a door or window open, and she gets out?" I couldn't quit worrying about Squeaky, but somehow I sensed that if God had led this far, he wasn't going to let me down in the matter of my cat, and he didn't want me to back out of the opportunity that had opened for me.

When I returned to the car, I told Pastor Meager that I had decided to go. He took me shopping for clothes and toiletries, and the next day he drove me all the way to Northern California, where I was supposed to embark on a new adventure in trusting God.

Chapter 20

As I looked around the campus where AFCOE was located, my fears were all confirmed. This was not a place where I would feel comfortable.

I saw a lot of fresh-faced kids who'd probably just graduated from a Christian high school and had probably never so much as taken a sip of beer, let alone experienced the drug-fueled, sex-crazed world I had come from.

I didn't even want to get out of the car. "I can't stay here," I told Larry. "Just let me go back with you."

He wasn't one to take no for an answer easily. "We've come all this way. Let's at least go meet some of the instructors, fill out the papers, maybe take a look around."

We went inside and met with John, the program director. "I don't belong here," I told him right off.

"Tell me a little about yourself," he responded.

After I'd told him a bit about my rough background, Larry said, "Nico has a special mission for the Lord, I believe. Nico, why don't you share your Spoken Word 'God's Soldier' with John?"

"Yes, please do. I'd like to hear it," John said.

Whenever I'm called upon to share the Spoken Word, I consider it both a privilege and a responsibility, so of course I couldn't turn down that request.

The message begins like this:

I am so honored to say

That I am one of many of God's soldiers.
And just like each and every one of you
I am in a continuous battle
Against the poverty, the disease and all the worldly sin
It is now and forever my most honest opinion
That none of us before or since has said anything that in the
Holy Bible has not yet been written.

So please take a good long look at me
And soon you will see
I am not the one disrespectin'
No, on the contrary I am so grateful for all I've been hearin'.
So thank you, each and every one of you for taking the time to
listen
To one of God's Soldier's opinion

It is a long poem that takes me more than five minutes to recite, and John listened intently down to the very last line where I affirm that

Until this war is over,
I am honored to say
That I was chosen to be
One of God's soldiers.

John sat quietly for a long moment when I had finished. He seemed to be studying me, considering how to respond. Finally he said "Nico, that is amazing, and I believe that God has indeed called you to be one of his soldiers."

He sat back in his chair then and jotted something on a notepad on his desk, then said, "I've got to be honest with you. We've never had anyone quite like you in our program here. Most of the young people who come have a pretty tame, conservative Christian background. But I sense that God has especially called you to be here."

"I'm not so sure," I said. "I don't think I'd fit in. I get really uncomfortable in crowds."

"Nico, I think God is calling you to be here," John said. "But we need to have an understanding before we accept your application. We can't have you glorifying your past life to the students, understood?"

"There's nothing glorious about it, sir. That's the last thing I would want to do."

"We'll let you pretty much run your own program, work with you on any special needs you have. Just promise me you won't hurt anybody—physically or spiritually." He was looking at the "TAKE THAT" tattoos on my knuckles.

"I wouldn't do that, sir. But you gotta understand, I just don't think I can stay here. I just won't fit in."

Larry was still determined not to let me say no to what he saw as more than just a fantastic opportunity. In his spiritual insight, he knew that I needed to stay there. He knew it wouldn't work out well for me to stay long with my father and his wife, and he had seen the only other place that had opened up for me—a dungeon-like apartment in Hollywood where I would constantly face the temptation to fall back into my old ways. "Why don't you go down to the dorm—see where you'd be staying—if you decide not to leave," he urged.

That was definitely not something I wanted to do, but since Larry had put so much effort into getting me there, I couldn't turn him down.

As soon as I got to the dorm, I knew for sure I wasn't going to stay. I could feel the walls closing in around me as I saw other students, clean-cut with smiling faces, moving in. Young guys and girls who hadn't experienced anything of life yet. Not my crowd—they made me feel queasy. People were talking and laughing, and I thought I was the butt of their jokes. I turned around and headed out the door, but then that pesky little voice started repeating its mantra, "Remember your promise...Remember your promise."

I decided I'd better at least peek into the room I had been assigned.

When I opened the door and saw bunk beds, that settled it. Promise or no promise, I was heading for the exit.

I didn't even notice that there was someone in the room until I heard a man's voice. "Hi, I'm Mike. You gonna be my roommate?"

"No," I responded without even thinking. "I'm actually leaving, not going to stay."

"Oh, too bad. I think you'd really like it. This is my second time here. I started the program last year, but I had to leave—got a blood clot in my leg and had to have surgery to have it removed."

I stared at Mike. He was no fresh-faced kid. In fact he was about my age and looked like he'd been around the block quite a few times.

"Really—a blood clot in your leg."

"Yeah, I was real heavy into crystal meth for a long time, really messed me up."

"What—you—man, what a coincidence! Look at my leg." I rolled up my pants-leg and showed him the bulging veins there, caused by blood clots from my days as a fighter.

"Man, yours look a lot worse than mine did. I had to have surgery last year—that's why I'm here now, back for my second try."

My head had been swimming before, now I almost felt like I was going to fall over.

"You were into crystal meth?"

"Not just using, I was dealing. Only by the grace of God am I here today. I almost died so many times."

"You aren't going to believe this, but that's my story too."

"I'd say the Lord put us together for a reason, wouldn't you, roomie?" Mike said.

As I looked at Mike and considered what he'd told me about himself, I remembered that I had told God that I'd be his soldier if he'd let me save myself by saving others. Mike seemed like the kind of person God would like me to minister to.

"Well, I've got to have the top bunk, then."

"No problem, bro."

"I'll be back in a bit, then," I said, closing the door and

heading down the hall that a few minutes earlier had seemed to be closing in around me. The walls had a totally different feel now—maybe they were even opening out into a bright, new future. "Okay, okay," I said to the voice that had been reminding me of my promise. "I'll give it a try."

When I got back to the office, I thanked Larry for bringing me and told him I'd decided to stay.

"Praise the Lord!" he said, and then helped me move my things into the dorm room.

Chapter 21

When I had given myself over to the side of darkness, the powers on that side of the battle were warm and welcoming. Somehow I found acceptance and a place to live wherever I went.

To be honest, I didn't expect to find that kind of acceptance and warmth in the Christian world. I'd seen and heard enough preachers in my day that I expected the Christians I was now associating with to be judgmental and condemning, looking down their noses at me because of all the bad choices I'd made.

But the people at AFCOE—students, faculty, and staff— did not live up to my expectations.

They were very different from what I had thought they would be.

The students treated me with respect and showed a great interest in learning from me—not learning how to become addicts, but learning about my experience, probing me for ideas about how to reach people in the depths of addiction.

Faculty members could tell that I was a fish out of water in their Bible classes and evangelism training. Everything they were talking about was totally new to me. One of the instructors, Eric, saw my distress and offered to spend an hour or two every week giving me basic instructions, tutoring me, so that I would be able to get more out of the class sessions. We spent almost every Monday afternoon together, and I learned a lot from him—not just facts and Bible verses, I learned a lot about life, and how to live as a Christian and a witness to what God had done in my life.

One of the class assignments was to go into a nearby town several afternoons per week to do door-to-door surveys of people's interest in spiritual topics, to try to find people who would be open to studying the Bible with us and eventually attending evangelistic meetings at a nearby church.

That assignment really troubled me. Places where I'd lived in recent years, if you went around knocking on doors, you'd probably be met by a dealer or a half-naked woman high on drugs. I didn't need that kind of thing in my life, so I managed to avoid carrying out that part of the assignment most of the time. John had, after all, told me I'd be allowed to pretty much run my own program.

Gradually I overcame my fears to the extent that I was able to do a few of those assignments, but honestly, I never became comfortable with that type of activity. While I realize people need to be able to reach out to their community in a variety of ways, that didn't seem to be my variety.

John and Eric and the rest of the staff lived up to John's promise to "work with me" in some amazing ways.

One example was when I started to obsess about Squeaky.

About halfway through the four-month program, I started waking up in the middle of the night worrying about my cat. I knew that my dad and step mother couldn't really relate to her—she wouldn't accept them as part of her life—wouldn't even let them touch her. I had always worried that she might someday get out through an open door or window, and if that happened they would have no way of getting her back inside.

Squeaky had come through thick and thin with me, and there were times when I felt she had actually saved my life when I was in the depths of my addiction. She represented innocence to me, and I couldn't bear the thought of something bad happening to her.

"I have to leave," I told Eric one day.

"What? Why?"

"My cat."

"What about your cat?"

I told him the whole story, and that I was waking up in the middle of the night worrying about her getting out and getting lost.

He tried to console me, telling me that God would help my dad keep Squeaky safe, but I told him I just couldn't quit worrying about her.

"But God has called you to be here, don't you believe that, Nico?"

"Yes, I know he has."

"But you're willing to leave, walk away from God's calling for the sake of your cat?"

"I have another idea," I said. I hadn't told him of the plan I had already schemed up. "Would you let me keep Squeaky with me in my dorm room?"

"We have a strict no animals policy in the dorm, I think you know that."

"But you could make an exception if you had to, right? I mean so that I can finish my training here."

"What about your roommate? The room's not big enough for the two of you and the cat. What if he's allergic?"

"Got that all worked out already."

He just stared at me, a smile toying with one corner of his mouth. He'd heard my stories about my success as a telemarketer. "Okay, Mr. hotshot salesman. Sell me on it."

"There's a guy down the hall that doesn't have a roommate. I talked to him and to Mike, and they're willing to room together so I don't have a roommate. Squeaky can be my roommate."

"How are you going to get her here?"

"My dad can put her on a plane."

"We'll have to get it approved by the administration. It's really that important to you? If the answer's no, you'd have to leave?"

"It's that important."

Amazingly, they approved my request. No one had ever been allowed to have a pet in the dorm before, but they felt strongly enough about my call to ministry, and my need to be there, that they bent the rules for Squeaky.

Now the challenge was to get Squeaky on a plane. Step one was for my dad to catch her and put her in a cage, then she had to be taken to the veterinarian to get clearance to fly.

Dad agreed to try, even though Squeaky had never let him touch her. When he called back a couple days later, he said the most amazing thing had happened. "I had towels wrapped around my hands so I wouldn't get scratched. But she just sat there, let me pick her up and put her in the cage. At the vet's office she sat with me, didn't put up a fuss, on the table in the exam room, she behaved like the perfect pet. I've never seen anything like it."

A few days later Squeaky flew into a nearby airport, and a friend took me down to pick her up. Everybody cooperated, and Squeaky—the only cat ever allowed in the dorm—was my roommate for the rest of the term.

That's just one example of how open and willing the staff at AFCOE was to work with me. And the way it worked out gave me assurance that my decision to stay had been the right decision.

Toward the end of my time there, Eric asked me one day if I would be willing to go and speak at a church where he had an appointment. Speaking in front of a large group of people came much more naturally to me than going door to door talking to individuals, so I accepted his invitation.

That appointment led to others, and soon I was speaking at one church or another almost every weekend, and that also helped to affirm my decision to stay at AFCOE and finish the course I had begun.

I learned a lot about the Bible while I was there, and I learned a lot about what it means to be a true Christian soldier—God's Soldier—sharing the love of God with people who may be very different from myself, but who are still people who are important to God. At the graduation ceremony in May, I was invited to share a Spoken Word, and I shared "God's Soldier."

After graduation I went back to stay with my father and stepmother, wondering just how God was going to open the doors for me to apply the things I had learned.

Start right where you are, with the people closest to you, was one of the things I'd been taught.

As I sat in the living room of Dad's home, looking across the room at him, I realized that meant start with Dad.

We had never been close, never talked much. I realized that a lot of the anger I had felt at the world and at myself stemmed from the early years when Dad had not been a very good father. "Reach out to the people closest to you," the thought kept echoing in my mind.

That was one of the toughest assignments I'd had so far. I retreated to my room and wrestled with the promptings.

For most of my life I had clung to my anger at my father, feeling justified. He hadn't been a good father, after all, by anyone's standards.

As I thought about it and wrestled with myself, I came to realize that my resentment had wormed its way down into the very core of my being. I had used it as the basis for excusing a lot of my own bad behavior. It's a common trick among addicts. Just blame your bad upbringing, and you don't have to take responsibility for your own stupid blundering.

One of the most important lessons I had learned at AFCOE was that God tells us to love our neighbor as we love ourselves. You can't do a very good job of loving your neighbor if you hate yourself.

I was still experiencing flashes of anger. I had learned to control them better, but I couldn't understand why little irritations sometimes made my blood boil. Then, as a picture of my father came up in my mind, I felt all that tension building inside me again.

If I was going to be God's Soldier, I needed to deal with my anger at my father.

But how? The more I thought about it, the more I

realized I actually cherished that anger, held onto it as a prized possession, used it as the basis of my self-justification. It was a key part of my psyche that I thought I needed in order to feel good about myself.

But in reality, it was making me feel bad about myself.

If I couldn't let that anger go, if I couldn't forgive my father, what kind of hypocrite was I for preaching the importance of forgiveness to others?

That's when the image of another Man on a Hill presented itself to me in all its dark, blazing glory.

The day the Man from the Tombs met Jesus, coming up the hill toward him, his life was transformed. And by the power of Jesus, he went to his neighbors whom he had done so much against, and told them what Jesus had done for him, how his life had been transformed by forgiveness for his past.

Because of what Tomb Man did, the next time Jesus came into that territory, large crowds came to hear his message. The whole region was transformed by the message of hope and forgiveness Jesus had brought to one man.

Later, though, Jesus himself was the Man on a Hill.

The Hill called Calvary.

He had been beaten and tortured far more viciously than anything I had ever experienced.

He was dying, with nails driven through his flesh by sadistic soldiers.

Did he harbor anger at them?

Did he use that as justification for calling down plagues on them?

No. What he did was offer them forgiveness. The very men who had beaten and tortured him, and were now subjecting him to a slow, agonizing death.

The vision of Calvary, the Man on a Hill, dying for the sins of the world, dying for my sins, dying for my father's sins, offering forgiveness to the cruelest of men, broke me. Tears streamed down my face.

How could I hold onto my anger at my father, when Jesus, on that hill, wanted nothing more than to forgive me, forgive my father, and forgive anyone who would believe in him and accept that forgiveness?

My heart rebelled at the thought of releasing its long-cherished rage. But gradually, over time, I made peace with myself.

Then it was time to make peace with my father.

"Dad," I said to him one night after dinner, "can we talk?"

"What about?"

"I, uh, I just want you to know that, well, we've never really been close, you know. And I guess, well, I've never really forgiven you for some of the things that happened when I was a kid. And I just want you to know that I've decided to let all of that go. I'm not going to hold any of that against you anymore. I realize I need to forgive others so I can forgive myself."

He looked at me like he didn't know what I was talking about.

"Whether you remember the things that happened or not, I want to forgive you Dad, and I want to ask your forgiveness. I know there's been a lot of times I haven't done right by you, and I'm sorry."

He smiled an odd smile, like he wanted to make a joke out of what I was saying. He clearly wasn't comfortable with this kind of talk.

"Will you forgive me, Dad?"

"Well, uh, yeah, sure. If it's important to you."

"That's all I needed to hear. Thank you, Dad. And please know that I forgive you, too."

He shrugged and looked down at the floor, then finally looked up. "Thanks, I guess. Thanks, Nico."

We didn't hug or get all teary-eyed with each other, or anything like that, but I felt truly liberated by the conversation. The weight of anger I had carried with me for so long had been lifted off my shoulders at last.

I gave him a Bible then, and invited him to begin reading it. Since then I know he has started attending church again.

The words "I forgive you" were hard to say, but it's easier to say the words than to actually empty all the resentment out of your heart. But I can honestly say that today I no longer harbor anger at my father. The past is the past. As God's Soldier I need to be advancing, always looking ahead for the next opportunity to share the forgiveness provided by the Man on a Hill, Jesus, with those who desperately need it.

Chapter 22

What was next for God's Soldier?

I had sensed a calling to reach out to the broken and downtrodden with the good news that there is a God in heaven who cares very much about them.

I'd been affirmed in my calling by Pastor Meager and others.

I'd been through a crash course in evangelism at AFCOE.

I'd been affirmed in my speaking ministry by the responses of people when I took appointments at several churches.

I had cleared up issues from my past that would stand in the way of being able to effectively present the message of God's forgiveness to those I would be called to minister to.

But now I was just sitting around my father's place, wondering what was next. Should I be out looking for a job? The two things I thought I could get work in were sales and acting. As I thought about my previous work in sales, I saw red flags all over the place. I hadn't really become successful until I'd learned how to tell the customer just exactly what he or she wanted to hear—not necessarily being outright deceptive, but perhaps not sharing everything they might want to know about the product I was touting. I didn't feel ready to face the temptation to be less-than-honest and above board in everything I did.

Acting seemed like it might be an option. I'd actually

been contacted by my agent recently about playing a role on a TV show, but that hadn't worked out, and as I thought more about it, I realized I didn't feel ready to deal with all the ego issues that had dragged me into the gutter before.

"Lord, you called me to be your soldier. Where's the battle? Where do you want me?" I prayed.

Then one day my phone rang, and it was Pastor Meager.

"Can you come to the Southern California Conference Office in Glendale next week? I have some people I want you to meet."

What would be the point of saying No to him? I'd probably end up doing it anyhow. "Sure," I said.

So, there I sat a few days later, in an office building, in a conference room, across the table from three gray-haired, conservative-looking men in business suits. Pastor Meager was there, and Pastor Larry Caviness, the president of the Southern California Conference of Seventh-day Adventists, the sisterhood of churches that Meager's church belonged to. The third man was Rick Roethler, one of the ministerial leaders for the conference.

Boy did I feel out of place. I felt like I had no business being in the same room with them.

Pastor Meager introduced me as a man with a powerful testimony to whom God had given tremendous gifts for reaching a group of people that the church might not be able to reach otherwise. "So, what's your story?" Pastor Caviness asked in a way that conveyed his genuine interest in what I might say.

I told them how God had spoken to me and redeemed me from the abyss I had dug myself into, and I shared one or two of my poems with them.

They all listened intently, asking a few questions along the way, then Pastor Caviness looked right into my eyes and said, "You know, Nico, I have a real heart for the lost. There are people out there that would never consider darkening the door of one of our churches, people sunk in the kinds of sins you indulged in. The church has no way of touching their lives, for the most part. But I sense that the

Lord has called you to that kind of mission—to reach out and touch the downtrodden and broken."

"That's exactly what I feel called to do," I affirmed. "I'm just not sure how to do it right now. I'm just living with my father, waiting for the Lord to open the next door for me."

"Thank you so much for coming today, Nico. There are tens of thousands of young people, just within our own denomination, that need to hear your story, need to meet someone like you as they are making life-changing decisions. You may be the one the Lord has sent to us to help us reach out in new ways to those young people. Let us pray about it, talk it over with church leaders, and see if there isn't some way that we can help you fulfill your calling."

Pastor Meager walked out of the room with me. "I think the Lord is moving," he told me. "I sense that there may be a door opening for you here. Keep it in your prayers, okay?"

"Sure," I said.

I drove back to my father's place with a renewed sense of hope and determination that I would, somehow, find a way to put the gifts God had given me to use in ministry.

A few days later Pastor Meager was on the phone again. "The Lord didn't just open the door for you, he kicked it down, Nico!"

"What do you mean?"

He then proceeded to tell me that a vote had been taken for several church organizations to contribute funds toward supporting my ministry for the next three months.

I was overwhelmed by the offer. On the one hand it was a fantastic opportunity. On the other, it would involve a lot of hard work and constantly opening up to larger groups of people about the many follies I had fallen into.

But what else could I do? I was the one who had asked the Lord to open new doors for me. I was the one who was traumatized at the thought of going back into sales or acting.

This, obviously, was the door the Lord was opening for me. And so I agreed.

With the support of the churches, and with the help of Pat and Mike, two men that I had met at AFCOE, I was able to begin putting together God's Soldier Ministries, a nonprofit organization dedicated to reaching out to troubled youths and others to help them avoid making the kind of mistakes that led me into the abyss.

The three of us began taking speaking appointments at churches and schools, sharing my story and staying afterward, usually for several hours, counseling young people and answering questions.

As word spread about Nico the Dragon, who was now a soldier in the army fighting against the old serpent/dragon called Satan, invitations to speaking engagements began pouring in, almost faster than we could fulfill them.

It was exciting to see how the Lord was opening doors, but it was also challenging and exhausting. People may think, because I'm writing this book now, and because I speak in churches and youth gatherings on a regular basis, that I get some sort of joy out of sharing my past.

In reality, it's like ripping open old wounds every time I have to stand in front of a group and tell them about all the foolish things I did. Only by the grace of God can I keep doing it over and over again. It never gets any easier.

Several really important, exciting things developed out of the time I was sponsored by the churches to go from place to place. Actually, they didn't support my ministry for only three months. Seeing the results we were having, they kept extending the time a few months at a time for a total of 18 months!

During that time Pastor Meager introduced me to a study program called Celebrate Recovery, which helped me understand myself, my addictive behavior, and my dependence on God much better.

Altogether I was able to share my testimony with more than 10,000 people in dozens of different places. In one of the places I met a man who had worked in the prison system for thirty years. He came up to me and said, "You know, I've never heard a message quite like yours—the way these young kids really relate to you. You should get a volunteer pass that would let you get into juvenile halls and other jails and minister there.

With his help I applied for the pass, not realizing it would take almost a year for all the background checks to be completed. In the meantime he helped me get into one of the juvenile facilities in downtown Los Angeles to speak.

When I got there the people in charge said they didn't think there was much point in my talking to the kids. "They don't really want to be here listening to anyone. It's almost their mealtime. You're going to have a hard time getting their attention."

"I'm not here for myself," I replied. "I feel it's a divine appointment. Let me talk to them and see what happens."

I don't take any personal credit for what happened that day, but not only did the kids listen, they plied me with questions afterwards, and every one of them expressed an interest in either rededicating themselves to Christ, or dedicating themselves for the first time.

The second time I accepted an appointment in a juvenile facility, I intended to take projection equipment with me to share a video in the chapel, but forgot part of my equipment. When I met with the people in charge of the facility, they said the only other option was to go right into where the young people live and talk to them one-on-one there. "We usually don't do that," the chaplain said. "But I feel impressed that if any of the ministries that come here could pull that off successfully, it would be yours."

The chaplain led me down into the area known as the pods, where the detainees live and eat and shower—spend all their time except when they are let out into the exercise area.

As we entered their domain, I felt like I was involved in frontline, in-your-face spiritual warfare. These guys are on their own turf, and the chaplain all of a sudden comes in and says he has a special guest. "We were going to have you go down to the chapel—some of you obviously didn't want to go—but we've got a DVD here, and we're going to play it.

This guy has a powerful, powerful testimony, and it's something you need to hear."

The kids were looking at me like, "Okay, what you think you got for me that I haven't heard before? I've heard it all before, you know!"

I thank God that I had that DVD with me. To explain where it came from, I first need to tell you about another of the really amazing things that has developed and brought tremendous blessings to my ministry.

Coming out from under the haze of addiction has been a slow and painful process for me. I feel like there is still so much missing from my life because of the damage I've done to myself through drug abuse. I mentioned earlier that one of the most troublesome parts of my continuing struggle to return to a normal life is the difficulty I have establishing normal, caring relationships.

About two years ago I began to pray earnestly about this, and I remember one night in particular when I pled with God, "Lord, you know how alone I feel. Is it just possible, in your all-seeing wisdom, that there is a woman out there who is enough like me that she could understand me and become a part of my life? Not just any woman, but one with a broken past like mine, who has decided to put God first in her life now. Lord, if there's someone like that out there for me, could you show her to me? And soon?"

The very next day a friend invited me to go with him to the Praise and Worship service held at CBS Studios that evening and share a Spoken Word with the group there.

I accepted his invitation, and it was there that I saw the woman I believe God was leading me to. There she was, sitting in the second row, praising God with her arms lifted in the air—the most beautiful woman I had ever seen. And I could tell that she was beautiful on the inside as well as on the outside.

I knew that if I could just get acquainted with her, God would lead us on from there, so as she started to walk out after the program, I hurried to catch up with her and called out loudly, "Hello!" It was all I could think to say. My mind was a muddle. The catalog of a thousand pickup lines I'd used in my bar-cruising days was gone, and I sensed that none of them would impress this woman anyhow.

I got her attention, and she turned and smiled. "Hi, I'm Nico," I said.

"Holly," she replied, extending a hand.

"I saw you there in the second row and wanted to meet you. Any chance you could stay for a minute and visit?"

"Sure," she said, and her smile made my heart skip a beat.

We talked there by the entrance until the security guard came by to close things up, then went out into the parking lot. I was so enthralled with Holly that I didn't even notice how cold it was outside. Later she told me she thought she was going to freeze that night, but she didn't complain. The longer we visited, the more I came to realize that she is just as beautiful on the inside as on the outside. She's an actress who rescues hurt and unwanted dogs off death row—that's her soft side in action. But she's no pushover. She can throw a mean punch—and take them too—in the boxing ring of all things!

Could it be that God had answered my prayer that quickly—that this was the woman who was enough like me that she could understand me and we could develop an ongoing relationship? I had to find out. I called her and texted her constantly for the next several days, and finally asked her out to dinner.

We went to one of my favorite haunts—The Oyster Bar—in the San Fernando Valley. I wanted to take her there because Chris, one of my closest friends through all the years, has tended bar there for decades, and I wanted him to tell Holly a little bit about me. Chris did me proud, not only telling her about my past, and how low I had fallen, but also testifying to how proud he was of me for getting sober and getting involved in trying to help others avoid the pitfalls that had taken me down.

After dinner we stood outside the restaurant for a long time, visiting again, and I learned more—and I became even more convinced that my prayer to meet a woman with a background enough like mine that she'd be able to understand me had indeed been answered. Holly told me that, like me, she had been verbally and physically abused as a child. Then when she was a teenager, her parents threw her out, and she ended up in the arms of an abusive boyfriend who beat her almost to death. Three months after she left him, he actually did kill his next girlfriend.

While we were in the restaurant, I noticed the tattoo she had on her arm. "Guard your heart above all else, because it determines the course of your life," it said—a verse from the biblical book of Proverbs. Hmmm... Isn't that what I had thought I was doing during all those years when I was drowning my pain with drugs and alcohol—not letting people get close enough to me to hurt me?

Someone had once told me that when you've been an addict and you finally get sober, that's when you'll find your soul mate. The longer we talked, the more convinced I became that I had just found mine. And I still believe it to this day. Holly has become the most important person in my life, and I believe she always will be.

As we were talking, she mentioned in passing that she loved building websites.

"You're kidding?" I said.

"No kidding."

"I was just thinking today about how badly I need a website for the ministry I'm starting."

"Count me in," was her immediate response. "I'd love to build a website for you if it will help to glorify God."

That gave us a good reason to keep meeting on a regular basis—not that I wouldn't have found a reason even if we weren't working on a website! I was smitten. I knew that this was the woman God wanted to be in my life, and as we worked together on the website, we came to understand each other better, and developed a close and loving relationship.

We're agreed on many things, one of the most important of which is that until I get my health and emotional issues that are the result of so many years of abusive living fully resolved through the restoring grace of God, and until we feel ready to marry and actually take vows in front of God, our relationship will remain chaste.

It's difficult to imagine that a man like me, accustomed to playing the field among a very loose-living group, could actually abide by those standards, but by the grace of God that's the way it's going to be.

Holly has been able to help me understand addiction and its results more clearly, because of her own involvement with Alcoholics Anonymous and Al Anon. We struggle with the question of where our relationship will go if I am not fully restored from the results of meth abuse and never become able to form the sort of emotional and spiritual bond that a married man and woman need to have. If that is the case, we will simply have to live with it. If my experience can help just one person decide not to start down the destructive path I pursued, that will be some consolation.

Holly has been amazing—sticking closer to me than anyone ever has. She makes phone calls, she created a logo and business card, and is working on developing apparel and other products that will help support the ministry through sales.

And she was the one who painstakingly researched and pursued leads until she found enough video clips about my past and present to put together a DVD that I can use to get the attention of people when I go to places like juvenile detentions centers, and even churches.

I call Holly my Lady of the Light. Light seems to emanate from everything she does. It was the DVD that she put together for me that I played for the young men at the juvenile hall.

Something about seeing me as I was before my addiction, then hearing my story of falling into the abyss and being rescued only by the grace of God touches young people's hearts, even the hearts of hardened gang members and drug dealers.

After showing the DVD, I shared my personal testimony of how God had worked in my life and shared some of the Spoken Word with them.

The effect was electric. The chaplain couldn't believe how positively the kids responded to me, and that is how an extremely important phase of my current ministry was opened up. I now have a pass that will allow me to enter into any of the 16 juvenile detention facilities run by Los Angeles County at will—it's the largest, most diverse juvenile correction system in the United States.

Over the coming months my ministry will be focusing largely on reaching out to troubled teens who've hit a rough spot on the road of life. The chaplain overseeing ministry in all of these facilities is dedicated to helping kids find a better way of life and break out of their downward spiral, once they've finished their time as detainees, and I will play an important part in helping him reach that goal.

I feel so honored that God has called me to be a soldier for him. He is the one who opens doors for me—often in ways I couldn't possibly do myself. That happened in a totally unexpected way when I spoke at the Victory Outreach church in Eagle Rock, California in 2014. The pastor there, Pastor Augie Barajas, asked me to get involved with the rehabilitation center the church runs, so I volunteered for a three-month internship there.

Try to imagine what that was like for me, if you will. I like to put it this way: *Overnight I went from making altar calls to cleaning bathroom stalls.* This came about at a time when I was just beginning to catch a glimpse of what great things God had in store for me as I served him. I thank God that Pastor Augie, who had begun his ministry by starting a church in Hollywood, looked at me, saw that I was in danger of falling back into the trap of trying to be a celebrity, and he knew just what I needed.

I had just returned from a cross-country trip to speak at a large youth gathering where the response had been phenomenal. After that trip to Florida I began to sense that God was going to use me to do far greater things than I had ever imagined. That sort of thinking can go to your head, no matter how devoted you are.

So, going from that sort of success to the humbling experience of living in a group home for recovering addicts was no doubt just exactly what I needed.

I entered Victory Outreach's intensive program where people right off the street are brought in and helped in their struggle to get free of drugs and bad associations that have dragged them into the same sort of abyss I had escaped from. It's a highly-disciplined regimen of worship, Bible study, and separation from the things of the world. No TV, no radio, no telephones, total devotion to work and spiritual training.

But after just a few weeks there I developed a serious health problem. My many years of martial arts training and fighting had done serious damage to my legs, and I had huge, bulging varicose veins, particularly on my right leg. While I was interning at Victory Outreach, I developed a life-threatening case of blood clots and phlebitis and had to be rushed to the hospital, where I underwent emergency surgery to remove the affected veins and deal with blood clots that could have killed me.

When I was ready to be released from the hospital, I had to choose where to go, and I chose to go back to Victory Outreach to finish my internship. Although I was in serious pain and barely able to walk, I didn't want to be untrue to my commitment. For the next two weeks I wasn't able to participate in many of the activities there—I was still bedridden. But God opened the door for me to soldier on for him even in that situation. My bed was just down the hall from a bed where men who were going through withdrawal from addiction were confined as they underwent treatment.

I knew what these men were going through, and God was able to use me, in my own confinement, to speak to them and help them walk through that lonesome valley to victory.

When my internship was completed, Pastor Augie urged me to join Victory Outreach's ministry full time, but I've sensed God's call for me to continue to work independently with God's Soldier Ministries, focusing for now on opportunities to reach troubled juveniles.

Exactly where this path will lead isn't always clear, but this much I know for sure: The rest of my life is dedicated to redeeming people, young and old, from the clutches that ensnared me for so long.

In this battle, to quote a famous warrior, we have only just begun to fight.

I feel like my life is a flower that was all closed up in the darkness of night, that has been supernaturally opened by the light of the gospel. It is still just a bud, just beginning to spread its petals.

What beautiful things does God have planned for my future?

I can hardly wait to see!

One day it has been promised
We will never again be alone, broken, hungry, or cold.
But we never know where or when
Our last chapter has been told
So please hold on
It's always darkest before the dawn!

Nico's Life Today
Words from Those Who Know Him Well

John Villa, Supervising Deputy Probation Officer, Los Angeles County, California

I have personally witnessed Nico speak to our minors on at least two occasions, and each time I have seen him reach youth like no other volunteer I have witnessed in my 26-year career as a Probation Officer, and we have had athletes, actors, and well-known celebrities among our volunteers. This is evidence that Nico's ministry is blessed by God in a very special way that does not require a human-based platform of fame or prestige. . . .

In my industry minors have a good eye for people who genuinely want to help them, and in the few times that I have seen Nico witness to our minors, I can easily see that they know that his heart is genuine and in the right place.

Chaplain Cedric Brown of Chaplain's Eagles, Los Angeles

One of the things about the young people in our institutions is that they come in with a feeling of hopelessness. And because of hopelessness, they don't feel confident that they can overcome their circumstances. They believe that the environment they come from is never going to change, so that they are doomed to repeat the same things over and over and over again.

So when you have someone like Nico who comes in and introduces himself and shares the experiences he's had—how he's been on top and on the bottom—and how God intervened and came and rescued him from himself, the young people can relate to that. . . .

Nico's video gets their attention because first of all he's showing who he was. But it's his openness and transparency in sharing how low he went that really makes a difference. . . .

He shows them that even though it seemed that he had everything that anybody could ever want, the main ingredient that was missing in his life was a direct relationship with God. I thank the Lord for a brother like Nico who has decided to give back and to make a difference in lives through his own testimony, establishing his own relationship with God and then deciding to be an ambassador for God.

Pastor Augie Barajas, Victory Outreach Church, Eagle Rock, California

The first time we met, he shared some of his Spoken Word, so I invited him to speak at our church. I was really blessed by the message in his words, and since we both had been involved with martial arts, we had something in common and developed a close friendship. . . .

One day I asked him how deep he wanted to go with the Lord, and he said he wanted to go all the way in serving God. At that point I told him he needed to go into our men's home, which is a place where people coming off addictions live for a year in a very disciplined program. Living there would be a great lesson in humility for a man like Nico who had been a celebrity and a shot-caller all his life. I didn't expect him to say Yes, but he did. . . .

I started my church in Hollywood in 1976, so I've dealt with celebrities before—they would never last in a program like this, but Nico stuck it out.

Then one day they told me Nico had been rushed to the hospital. I didn't know how bad it was until Holly called and told me there was a blood clot going from his legs toward his heart. . . .

Later the doctor told me he thought he was going to

have to amputate Nico's leg, but they were able to save it, despite all the damage that had been done to his veins through the years of fighting and drug abuse.

When Nico was released from the hospital, his father was there to take him to his home, but Nico insisted on going back to the Victory Outreach home, to finish his time there. He couldn't stand, couldn't walk, but still he wanted to be true to his commitment. I was amazed. After he recuperated there, he went right back to work sweeping and cleaning, just like all the other residents. One of the last times I saw Nico at the home, he was down on his hands and knees in the parking lot, cleaning weeds out of the cracks so the lot could be repaved. I said Praise God! God can really use this man. I feel honored that he calls me his spiritual father. I hope that someday soon he will be able to travel to many of the countries where we have outreach to the inner city, because God has given him a message that reaches people and changes lives.

Chaplain Lawrence Foy, Optimist Home, Eagle Rock, California

Nico Hill is a passionate and committed believer in advancing the Kingdom presence of God. His words are simple, yet powerful and life-transforming. I have literally seen youth give their life over to Christ upon hearing Nico's message. He exhibits a unique way of incorporating his personal story of rising to stardom and great success in the world of fighting, along with his plunge into the abyss and failure through self-destructive behavior. In the darkness of the abyss, however, Nico informs us that Jesus lifted him off of the canvass of the abyss and gave him reason to fight again. He now wages a new fight as a soldier for Jesus Christ—sharing the love and forgiveness of Jesus to young people and to anyone who is willing to listen. I encourage you to listen to the "Spoken Words" of Nico—and you will be forever changed.

Matt Burch, TV personality from Operation Repo, and long-time friend.

I met Nico "The Dragon" around the year 2000, and he and I used to hang together a lot. We were kindred spirits, and by that I mean we liked to get into the same kinds of trouble. Don't get me wrong, we weren't really bad guys. We're both pretty decent fellows at heart, but we were caught up in the fast Hollywood life of wine women and song. . . .

These days I'm happy and proud to see that Nico is using his God-given gifts for a positive purpose. When he speaks, people listen. He has a way of presenting the gospel that gets right down to the heart of things and touches the hearts of his listeners. He can reach kids who would never listen to a preacher with less street cred.

David "Shark" Fralick, television and movie actor and long-time friend

I am so impressed and so excited to see the way that Nico is taking his life experiences, both the good and the bad, and using them as a positive influence for young people today. When he goes into a facility for troubled teens, he gets their attention like nobody else, because he's "been there and done that!" His testimony crosses barriers, he's accepted by people from all backgrounds. I've watched him talk to young people—gang members, drug dealers, prostitutes, the down-and-out, people one step from prison or death. They all respect him, as I do. I'm honored and grateful and lucky to have him in my life. He has a charisma that attracts them to him, but more than that, they know he's not just some preacher telling them what not to do. He speaks from the real world—the kind of world they live in—and he's courageous enough to open up about all the mistakes he's made, how he got on the wrong path, and where it led him.

Pastor Larry Caviness, president of the Southern California Conference of Seventh-day Adventists

"Is this not a brand plucked from the fire?" (Zechariah 3:2). Nico is a modern example of this verse. First he was plucked out of the fire that consumes with evil and darkness, then he was plunged into the fire that purifies, and now he ministers with the fire of the Holy Spirit that empowers him to be a living witness to what God has done in his life.

To learn about Nico's current ministry and see videos and read more about his work, please visit the web page www.godssoldierministries.org

During my years of drug abuse, most of my personal photos were lost or stolen, but here are a few that stayed with me from my fighting days. You might recognize some well-known fighters including Kimo, Benny Urquidez, Frank Dux, Oleg Taktarov, and Joe Charles.

Living in the fast lane in Hollywood made me feel like I had arrived. You may recognize Oscar De La Hoya, Gary Busey, Steven Bauer, and others here. Also my custom bike and my car The Beast under construction.

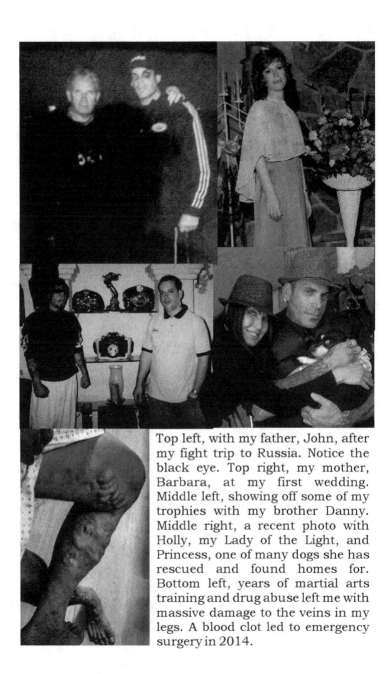

Top left, with my father, John, after my fight trip to Russia. Notice the black eye. Top right, my mother, Barbara, at my first wedding. Middle left, showing off some of my trophies with my brother Danny. Middle right, a recent photo with Holly, my Lady of the Light, and Princess, one of many dogs she has rescued and found homes for. Bottom left, years of martial arts training and drug abuse left me with massive damage to the veins in my legs. A blood clot led to emergency surgery in 2014.

FROM THE WRITER

When I was first approached about the idea of writing a book about a guy who had been an actor and cage fighter, then had tried to kill himself with illegal drugs, but had given his life to Jesus and was starting a ministry, I must admit that I was skeptical. I'd met enough burned out addicts in my life to make me doubtful that there was much there worth writing about.

"Just meet with him and see what you think," I was urged.

So I did. That first day we spent two or more hours together, and by the end of that time I knew there was a story worth telling here, about a man who had been touched in a remarkable way by the Spirit of God, who was now reaching out and changing lives in a powerful way.

Working with Nico to bring his story into print has been one of the most interesting and inspirational adventures of my life. You can't be around him for long without coming to realize that there is something special here. A special gift for presenting the gospel to anyone, anywhere, in a way that reaches down into the core of their being and challenges them.

I'm honored to have had this opportunity, and I know that God has great things in store for Nico as his story continues to touch more and more people around the world. His life, and his words, can bring the light of hope into even the darkest lives.

Other books by Ken Wade

Secrets of the New Age
Savage Future
There's Always Hope
The Orion Conspiracy
Back on Track
Jesus for a New Millennium
The Joy of Jesus
Del Delker
Journey to Moriah
Paul: A Spiritual Journey
Really Living-1
Really Living-2
Journey Through the Bible: Genesis to Job
Journey Through the Bible: Psalms to Malachi
Journey Through the Bible: Matthew to Revelation
Secret Corners
Bound by Blood